The American Lawyer

The American Lawyer

As He Was-As He Is-As He Can Be

By
JOHN R. DOS PASSOS

BeardBooks
Washington, D.C.

CONTENTS

CHAPTER I

CHAPTER II

CHAPTER III

CHAPTER IV

CHAPTER V

CHAPTER VI

CHAPTER VII

CHAPTER VIII

CHAPTER IX

CHAPTER X

THE

AMERICAN LAWYER.

CHAPTER I.

INTRODUCTORY.

It is assumed that what the people of the United States really think or want, as citizens, is expressed through the ballot box. In the interim of these official utterances, public thought is reflected, and more or less created, by the four great organs of public opinion,—the Pulpit, the Press, the Bar, and the Stage. I shall not undertake to estimate the relative value of each of these organs, as creative forces, in shaping the course and destiny of the nation, but it is impossible to discuss one without keeping them all in view. They are parts of a whole. They bear the same close relationship to each other that the nose, the ears, the eyes, and the throat, do to the head. Still each is capable of separate,

A   1

distinctive treatment; but it is only by acquiring a correct knowledge of them all, that one can fully comprehend the combined influence which these four organs may have upon existing affairs.

My subject is the Bar, but I must elucidate it, here and there, by brief reference to the Pulpit, the Press, and the Stage.

In a confederation of States like the one which we have established, with a written Constitution, it seems natural that the lawyers should predominate in the government. They framed the former instrument. They both make and interpret the laws. While this is said to be a government of the people, by the people, and for the people, it is not, perhaps, going too far to add,—subject to the lawyers. At least, the crude sentiments of the people, must be filtered through the lawyers, first as politicians, then as legislators, and afterwards as lawyers and Judges. The lawyers swarm in all of the departments of the National and State Government, and while they never act in public questions as an organized body—as a unit—their influence, in all branches of public and private life, is most profound and penetrating. It is, therefore, both the right and interest of the whole people to demand that lawyers should be intelligent, capable, honest, and devoted to the administration of justice. When hundreds of lawyers are turned out upon the community each year, to graze upon all of the pastures of public office; when they swarm in, and control, every branch of the government, executive, judicial and legislative, no question is of more importance to the people than to know whether this dominating class is living up to its true mission. Despite this palpable truth, the laity has paid no attention to the subject. Nor does the Bar make any full, real, introspection of itself.

"Know thyself" was the Delphian invocation. In every aspect of life, it is to be classed among the most important of commands. It has been overlooked, or neglected, by the lawyers in respect to their office. At least, no one has yet made public the results of an investigation of the profession. While the multitudinous treatises which legal writers have published, cover almost every inch in the extensive field of technical law, the important region of the lawyer's vocation seems to have escaped them. Apparently no lawyer has yet published the real nature of his calling— going from the top to the bottom of it. The reason is obvious. It is a subject more literary and general, than legal. It carries one far beyond precedent. He who ventures therein must be prepared to quit the sacred precincts of precedent and *stare decisis*, and depend upon ethics, and the natural conditions, which underlie human society.

When lawyers become authors, they are unable to free themselves from technical and professional restraints, and while their works have done something, to reduce the law to a science, within itself, yet its more comprehensive relations have escaped them. Hence the enormous importance of those aspects, which, while doubtless felt in a dim way, have hitherto received but little recognition as living forces in society.

But beyond all of this; when a lawyer undertakes an honest introspection of his profession, he is very apt to run into a confession. He must then say some ugly things about himself. Men do not like to confess, except to themselves. Hence, while many lawyers have doubtless ruminated upon the subject—covering with their mind's eye the same field which I am about to traverse—they have not screwed their courage to a point of putting their thoughts upon paper.

It is of the first importance to endeavor to ascertain, accurately, the due relation of lawyers to other interests of the community, and then to inquire if they have lived up to it.

What is a lawyer? What is his real mission? What relation does he bear to the government of which he is a citizen? What are his real duties to society?

Some technical books have been written about the obligations of lawyers. Warren published his lectures,[1] the broad title of which, if it had been sustained in the text, would have covered some of the ground gone over here; Forsyth's "History of Lawyers" is a most interesting historical review of the profession from remote periods; and Sharswood has contributed a little work on Professional Ethics. And there are several books on the lawyer's technical duties and liabilities.

Besides, narratives, lectures, and essays, without stint, have been written and published, covering legal romance and history, and all phases of a lawyer's life and of his relations to his client; but no one has raised the curtain upon the lawyer in his full relations to society. In all of their writings, one sees that the lawyer's vision of his calling, seems to have extended no further than to a contemplation of his duties to his clients, and to the courts. We look in vain for any adequate, distinctive, treatment of this subject, beyond this narrow view.

It is quite well understood that to his clients the lawyer is held to unexceptionable purity of conduct, and that he must be fair and honorable with the Court. These duties are imperishably

[1] "The Moral, Social and Professional Duties of Attorneys and Solicitors."

written upon the lawyer's mind. They seem to be a part of the milk of his education, which he unconsciously imbibes before entering upon the duties of his office.

The lawyers stop here in the survey of their mission, and as there is no course of instruction, or book, which opens to them their full duties, it is not surprising, that they start out in professional life, with a very inadequate knowledge of their calling. Fundamentally, they believe that, at the top and bottom of their professional career, they should serve their clients at all sacrifices, sometimes even of truth and justice.

Accordingly, I know of no occupation more interesting, than to attempt to hold up to the lawyer, a faithful picture of his real mission. It then will be seen, that a large number of the lawyers are delinquents to society, not with malice prepense, but from a failure to appreciate the real and full nature of their professional duties.

CHAPTER II.

THE GENEALOGY OF THE LAWYER.

THE profession of the law has been at all times, and in all countries, a favored and honored calling. This distinction, it appears, originally grew out of the superior knowledge of the lawyers. In England, the nobles and warriors of ancient times were ignorant of reading and writing, and if they did not look with absolute contempt upon these arts, they at least regarded them as effeminate and inharmonious with their lives. All knowledge was locked up in the breasts of Ecclesiastics, who acted in the multiform relation of priests, literati, moralists, and law advisers. It was then, as it should be (but is not) now, the man of superior mind and education controlled. But apart from direct historical data, lawyers are a necessary part of civilization. There must always exist, in connection with a government, a body of men whose business and training fit them as interpreters of law—standing, as it were, between the State and litigants, to see that proper application of laws, is made to individual disputes.

In England the law began to be cultivated as a separate study in the thirteenth century.[1] The lawyers gradually segregated themselves from the ecclesiastical system, and an independent order of their own was the consequence. Regulation of attorneys was made in the reign of Henry IV.

Reeves [2] puts it in this wise:

> "The Parliament began to make some provision for ordering *attorneys*, who had now become a very considerable body of men. Complaint had been made of the mischiefs arising from their ignorance and want of knowledge of the law; and therefore, to make sure of their qualifications, it was ordained by Stat. 4, Hen. IV, c. XVIII, that all attorneys should be examined by the justices, and by their directions their names should be put in a roll; they were to be *good and virtuous* and of good fame; and if they appeared to be such, they were to be received and sworn well and truly to serve in their offices, and especially that they make no suit in a foreign country; all other attorneys were to be put out, and such as were passed in the above manner

[1] See Pollock & Maitland's "History of English Law," Vol. I, page 211 et seq., 2d ed.

[2] "History of English Law," I, p. 422.

were to be put in their places by their *masters* (sic), that is, by their *clients*.

"It was enacted that when qualified attorneys died, or ceased to act, the justices might appoint others in their room, being *virtuous* and *learned*, and sworn as above mentioned.

"It was enacted, that if any attorney was found notoriously in default, of record, or otherwise, he should forswear the court, and never be received to make suit in any of the king's courts; this ordinance was also to be observed in the exchequer at the discretion of the treasurer and barons."

The lawyer first appeared as a friend and adviser of the court. He worked with the latter to sift out the truth and render justice. When the occupation of the lawyer, however, consisted in representing litigants before the courts for money, the intimacy, so to speak, between himself and the court began to weaken, and so far as his individual cases were concerned it was simply human nature, that his advocacy of his client's interests should overcome his independence, and that his usefulness, as a true friend of the court, should diminish. Originally, the client could not read or write; and notwithstanding that the law was simple and contained in a few books, the client did not understand it. Now the client can both read and write; but the law is complex and multifarious, and the client cannot pursue it, in all of its labyrinths, without a trained legal guide, and that legal guide very frequently knows not the way out of the woods himself, for the paths through adjudications, statutes, codes, and law treatises, are mazy and tangled.

It is a characteristic of the human mind to be faithful to a trust; to be over- rather than under-zealous in its performance. In all the varieties of affairs where individuals are compelled to repose confidence in others, the breach of it is the exception, not the rule. The lawyers are the most prominent illustrations of this truth. Fidelity, zealousness, untiring industry, and all kinds of personal sacrifices in the interest of the client, are their predominating traits. This has led them to excesses in advocacy—often to gross exaggeration of facts—and sometimes to crime. Inordinate zeal for clients, and ambition to win, are powerful stimulants to human energy, and often sweep away moral and legal barriers, which stand in the path of success. Human nature was very much the same in the thirteenth, as it is in the twentieth, century. The brakes were then applied to the illegal practices of lawyers as they are now; and a statute is cited, passed in King Edward the First's day (1275), threatening with imprisonment the "serjeant countor," or advocates guilty of collusive or deceitful practices.

The only importance of the above references is to show that at all times there has been a tendency on the part of lawyers, generally from excess of zeal, sometimes from greed or ambition, to overstep the limits of true professional bounds. They also serve to apprise the present Bar that all of the evils are not characteristic of this era.

The abuse of power and opportunities, and of unlimited confidence, is the primary sin for which the lawyers are answerable. What this power is, and when and how the confidence is bestowed, will be set forth in the subsequent chapters. But they chiefly arise out of their relation to the State, and not to their clients.

CHAPTER III.

IT is said that comparison gives definiteness
and clearness to thought, and that we never can
understand anything well, without comparing
it with something else.

I am drawing a line between the period before
and after the Civil War, and I put the old generation of American lawyers on the farther side,
and the new ones on this side of the line. I thus
institute a comparison which I think is happy.
I cannot speak with complete knowledge of the
old generation. I was not of it. It was gradually
disappearing when I became an apprentice to the
law. I gathered enough, however, from instruction and association, to speak with some authority
of the past. The fundamental difference between
the old and new régime of lawyers is this: the
great aim of the old lawyers was to master the
elements of law; they depended upon an eloquent
presentation of their causes; they stood nearer to

12

the courts than the lawyers of to-day; the judges had the time, and it was their pleasure, to listen to the advocates; "commercialism" did not exist; there were less legal tricks or technical legerdemain to resort to, because that dire plague of codification had not yet spread itself over the profession, and destroyed its science, as it existed under the common law, where, while form was strictly observed, the substance or merits of a controversy, were principally sought for.

The lawyers of to-day are case and code lawyers. The search for *principle* is subordinate to an investigation for a *precedent*. The right or justice, or the merits of controversies, disappear under a mass of irreconcilable decisions and forms. It requires a different kind of intellectual development to be a lawyer than it did in the days long gone by. The modern code lawyer is bright enough, and his wits, like the quills on a fretful porcupine, are always in full play. He knows little of elementary law, but he carries, as a soldier would a knapsack, a memory filled with sections of codes and adjudicated cases. A legal combat now consists of hurling provisions of the Code and "pat" precedents at each other. Hence the modern advocate's nose is always to be found in a digest, "case"-law accumulating so fast that he must have indices to search for his precedents. Poor soul! if he cannot find a precedent, he is in a terrible sweat. But he is resourceful and sophistical, and in the absence of his "authority" he begins to differentiate and distinguish, and he grinds away at the precedent of his adversary until it is whittled to nothing. If he is clever in his presentation, the courts generally follow him, and wipe out the old precedent by differentiation, and with a mock respect for *stare decisis*, pay as much attention to it, when it stands in the way of their latest convictions, as a court of last resort would regard a decision of a primary magistrate.

I must pause here to say a word in reference to the doctrine of *stare decisis*. It is a venerable principle in Anglo-Saxon jurisprudence. To-day, while there is an affected respect for it, there is often an actual departure from it, introducing manifold inconsistencies and confusion. It is a serious question whether the doctrine of *stare decisis* can be, now, strictly upheld. Under any conditions it necessarily dwarfed the intellect, and stifled moral convictions. No lawyer, or court, could accept a precedent, which he believed to be wrong, without a struggle, and with reluctance. The effort of the legal and judicial mind in these times is to differentiate it, and thus escape from its consequences. Whatever merit the doctrine possessed a century ago (and as a rule of property

it was great as fixing stability), precedents have
accumulated so fast that the mind is lost in a
maze of confusion in endeavoring to follow them.
When the law reports were few, and the precedents shone like bright stars, in the legal firma-
ment, and the lawyers knew and followed them,
as astronomers do the particular planets, the
application of *stare decisis* was easy and simple.
But now—it flitters between the thousands of
decisions as a phantom of the law—not as a
vital principle.

I will give a striking instance occurring in the
State of New York, which illustrates the condition of the doctrine of *stare decisis*, caused by
a multiplicity of decisions and legal reports.

In the case of *Williams* v. *Trust Co.*, decided
in May, 1892 [1] it appeared that the plaintiff had
pledged to the defendant certain bonds, as security for a loan under a collateral stock note, providing that in case of default in payment at the
time specified, defendant might sell the securities "in such manner as they in their discretion
may deem proper without notice." The note
was dated March 1st, 1884, and was payable
six months after date. The plaintiff's rights
were not foreclosed on the maturity of the loan,
but there were numerous interviews and com-
munications between the parties looking to the

[1] 133 N. Y. 660.

extension of the loan, and operating, as claimed by the plaintiff, as a waiver. Notwithstanding the efforts of the plaintiff, to have the question of waiver determined by the jury, as one of fact, the Court refused, and held that the defendants had the right to foreclose the pledge, without notice, at any time, after the maturity of the loan, unless the written agreement was in some way modified, and that the parties had not modified their rights by anything that occurred after the 1st of September, when the loan matured. The Court of Appeals sustained this view, and defeated the plaintiff, holding that the Court below committed no error, in not submitting the case to the jury.

This direct question came again before the Court in the case of *Toplitz* v. *Bauer*,[1] in January, 1900, nearly eight years after the preceding case. In that case the Court, contrary to its decision in the preceding case of Williams, held that the contract of bailment, whereby personal property is pledged, as security for a debt, is one of the class of contracts where *the mere indulgence on the part of the creditor by a promise to extend the time, or by his conduct, will effect a change in the duties and obligations of the parties to each other,* as prescribed by the original agreement, and that where the original contract

[1] 161 N. Y. 325.

under which property is pledged as collateral security for the payment of a note, permits a sale, public or private or otherwise, without notice to the pledgor, the right of the pledgee to so dispose of it, upon default in payment of the note, may be waived by agreement, declaration, or course of conduct on his part, which leads the pledgor to believe that a forfeiture will not be insisted upon without an opportunity given him to redeem, and no new or independent consideration is required to support the waiver, and that if, after having waived his right to a strict performance of the contract, the pledgee proceeds on the note, without notice, he is liable for damages occasioned thereby in an action of conversion.

Now the vicissitudes of the doctrine of *stare decisis* under present conditions were powerfully displayed in the above litigations. The case of Williams was controlling upon the court, in the latter case of Toplitz, but the court, consisting of a different personnel, did not remember its own previous decision, nor was its attention called to it in the points of counsel, on either side; and hence it proceeded to decide the Toplitz case on a new line of reasoning, in entire ignorance of its previous decision in the Williams case! A century ago such a precedent would hardly have passed unnoticed. .

B

Now which of these decisions is right, and which is binding? Naturally, or logically, the last decision. But, inasmuch as it was made without any knowledge of the previous one, the whole question apparently remains open. Yet thousands of dollars were lost by the unsuccessful litigant in the first case, and as much saved by the fortunate plaintiff in the second. Alas! for the uncertainty and instability of *stare decisis*.

This is only one illustration. I cannot afford space for others. No doubt they are within the recollection and reach of the Bar, and, unfortunately, in sufficient number to show how sensibly weakened the doctrines of *stare decisis* has become, by virtue of a multiplicity of decisions which cannot be unearthed, even by the most lynx eyed, or industrious precedent hunter.

These views are further illustrated in reading the decisions of the Supreme Court of the United States, and those of the highest courts of the individual States—say for the last twenty-five years. Such a mass of bad reasoning, illogical conclusions, disregard of the rule of *stare decisis*, contradictory statements, and an ignorance or contempt of the history and spirit of the Constitution of the United States, and of the several States; such a lack of knowledge of elementary law, and of the principles of jurisprudence, hardly can be imagined to exist. Let anyone, for example, undertake to enter into the extensive field of decisions, created by the interpretation of the Commerce Clause of the Constitution, since the Civil War, and if he does not emerge with a mind scratched and bleeding from the thousand thorns there existing, it is because he has no intellectual perception. That simple enactment, whose history is so well known to students of the American Constitution, has been so twisted and turned by the judicial minds which have grappled with it, that it can be said of it, as was repeated of the "Year Books"—a precedent can be there found on any side, of any subject, which anyone chooses to espouse. Legislative, and judge-made law, have accumulated so fast and thick, that elementary principles, buried thousands of feet deep under mountains of precedents, rarely can be brought to the surface. Courts are ashamed to confess that a precedent which they have made is wrong. It requires great courage to overrule a freshly made decision, and hence it is, as it were, "jumped." But I must return to my parallel. Legal practice, to-day, is fencing with the forms of the law, and most of the time the real issue is buried out of sight. The case of *Fogg* v. *Fisk* [1] is a good illustration. By the Code of Procedure of

[1] 30 Hun's Rep., p. 61, aff'd 93 N. Y. 652, 113 U. S., p. 713.

New York, under certain circumstances a party to an action may examine the other party before trial. The plaintiff applied for an order for the examination of the defendant. It was granted. The defendant appealed to the General Term of the Supreme Court. The order was sustained. Then he carried the cause to the Court of Appeals, which in turn affirmed the original order. The defendant was at his wits' end. He must submit to the examination. But his lawyers were equal to the emergency. They transferred the cause to the Federal Court, upon the statement that the defendant could not have a fair trial in the State Court. There was not the slightest ground, in fact, for the motion to transfer, because but few knew of the existence of the case, and those who did cared nothing about it. The affidavit that a fair trial could not be had, however, was not traversable under the then Act of Congress. The object of the transfer, was to avail of a decision of the Circuit Court of the United States, that the practice of examining a defendant before trial did not prevail in the Federal Courts. But the Circuit Court judge held, that the defendant could not cut off an examination, already begun in the State Court, by a removal to the Federal Court. The defendant then refused to answer; put himself in contempt; sued out a *habeas corpus* from the

Supreme Court of the United States, and that august tribunal set him free, holding that he escaped examination by removal. The case went to the highest court of the State and of the United States upon a mere question of form—of practice. When it had progressed to this stage, the defendant died, and not one word had ever been heard of the merits! Every practicing lawyer can furnish one or more similar stories.

What kind of a mental make-up must a lawyer possess, under these conditions, to attain prominence? He must be sharp, clever, wakeful, with the multifarious provisions of a Code constantly at his beck; a fresh, hot, precedent at his tongue's end; he must be quick of speech, bold, even audacious, in the choice of remedies; he must be a good business man, understanding the necessities of commercial development, and he must create, or make effective, the great schemes of present times, so that his clients will not be entangled in the meshes of modern legislation, which springs up as grass, every year, to entrap the unknowing. Real eloquence, and a knowledge of sound elementary law, have almost disappeared, and the lawyer is burdened by the incubus of form and statutes and codes, under which he staggers like Christian in the "Pilgrim's Progress," under the weight of his sins; not, like him, to have a happy deliverance from them, for when he cannot have recourse to them, he finds none in any other kind of mental equipment, or even in natural ability, or talent. They cut a small figure in his professional life. In a word, merits, justice, are not sought for. A judicial inquiry into the rights of parties means a search for "points" and forms and precedents.

A comparison between the past and present lawyer, is not disadvantageous intellectually to the latter. He has no less brains; no less natural intelligence; and he is a better business man, withal, than the lawyer of yore. Simply, he is armed with different weapons. Powder has given way to dynamite; the flint musket to the rifle of twelve cartridges; the cannon loaded at the muzzle and discharged every five or ten minutes, to the breechloader which automatically pours out its murderous fire every second. The lawyer now boldly enters into the business end of his client's transactions—he sells him prudence and experience, sometimes even usurping the client's discretion and judgment. In point of morals, I can discover little or no difference between the past and present lawyers. As a class, the lawyers always have been ready, to avail themselves of all the weapons at hand, to assist their clients in good or bad causes. It is a lamentable truth.   The honest and dishonest lawyers shelter themselves under the same pleas, that the law is uncertain, because of its multiplicity. Unfortunately it is more or less a chance.   A lawyer, therefore, has a technical answer ready, to sustain him in taking any case.   Codification has produced more material to aid dishonest clients than the common law supplied.   General business is greater—opportunities more frequent.   Hence, trickery, cunning, and pettifogging are more pronounced and visible.   I doubt, however, if, in proportion to actual numbers, and existing commercial conditions, the lawyers, as a body, are morally worse than their professional ancestors.

But let me proceed a step farther in the comparison.   In the United States the lawyers, down to the commencement of the Civil War in 1861, were the recognized social and intellectual aristocrats of the land.   They possessed all of the intelligence of the English lawyer, and at least an equal share of scholastic refinement and learning.   When, after the Civil War, Judah P. Benjamin, of Louisiana, went to London to practice law, he easily rose to the first position at the English Bar.   It was a point of pride with the American lawyer to be "up" in the best literature, ancient and modern.   A nice sense of professional honor, great pride in his calling, and the highest respect for the principles of the law, were the distinguishing features. There was a sharp difference between them in their conceptions of democracy as illustrated in the teachings of Hamilton, on the one side, and Jefferson, on the other; but predominating their party convictions was a deep faith in political, religious, and social freedom; a profound devotion to the Constitution, both in what it gave and secured, and in what it limited according to differing, but enlightened, interpretation. The lawyers of the past generation believed the Constitution was *adaptable*—those of the present regard it as *elastic*. This is an age of electricity. The people have neither the time, nor patience, to amend the Constitution. Hence, if prevailing thought demands a Federal law, the Constitution is stretched to uphold the necessary power—at the expense, of course, of the true Federal system. Stretched to a point when the rubber gives way, it touches centralization, but the courts are human, and generally follow prevailing opinion. The Congress, forsooth, has power to make greenbacks a legal tender, but no power to create a broad and fair income tax! Here is as beautiful a piece of inconsistency as can be found in our constitutional history. According to the best judgment of the profession, the very reverse is the law—Congress had no power in the former, but full power in the latter, case.

The profession of a lawyer in the United States, to continue, justly carried with it the right to occupy the highest social and political positions. A lawyer commanded respect and confidence. I remember, as a small boy, that, walking one day, some one pointed to a man whom he said was a lawyer. I distinctly recall the impression made upon me. I said, "There goes a man who knows everything," following Cicero's definition of an orator. This was the prevailing opinion of the world. It has not yet entirely faded out. *Then* it was pronounced; *now* it is indistinct.

The Bar has never been dangerous or exclusive; largely, perhaps, because it has never been unionized. No man, or party, ever dared to attempt to use the American Bar to advance selfish or sinister designs. Yet genuine patriotism among lawyers is, to-day, but feebly illustrated. I believe many of them would stretch the Constitution (Federal or State) until it cracked, to win a case.

The Civil War marks the commencement of an era of professional change—perhaps I am justified in saying, an intellectual decadence—in the Bar. There certainly was a transformation, from a profession to a business. Before that event, the position of a successful American advocate was regarded as the most honorable and splendid in civic life. It was the social *Ultima Thule*. It was the goal to which the intellectual and ambitious youths of the nation strove to reach by heroic efforts of study and self-abnegation.

The reason was plain. Eloquence was one of the principal attributes of the distinguished advocate, and while it was never cultivated as a separate art, as in Greece and Rome, the individual lawyer mastered it in his own way, guided by his own instincts and genius, and by such lights as he could borrow from successful contemporaries, and ancient and classic models.

The study of eloquence is unquestionably one of the most alluring, as it is one of the most ennobling, occupations in which the mind can engage.

> " As when of old some orator renowned
> In Athens or free Rome, when eloquence
> Flourished, since mute, to some great cause
>   addressed,
> Stood in himself collected, while each part,
> Motion, each act, won audience ere the
>   tongue
> Sometimes in highth began, as no delay
> Of preface brooking through his zeal of
>   right."

The aim of the orator being to vindicate right and justice, as the painted purpose of the chivalric knight of old was to protect and emancipate the oppressed, he necessarily must deeply inquire into the principles of truth, cultivate the graces of language, and train his mental and physical faculties, to be always ready to, resolutely and courageously, defend the causes placed in his hands.

The study of metaphysics and logic, of history, literature, languages, and poetry, is necessarily involved in the character of an orator. The great book of human nature must ever lie open before him. It has always been one of the most absorbing passions of man, to be able to stand up before his fellows and be listened to. It is a psychological felicity that perhaps preponderates all other ambitions. To-day it is the dominating passion of all Americans to talk. More oratory, illustrating every conceivable kind of rhetoric, true and false, is now heard in the United States in a week, when the legislatures are in session, than Athens or Rome listened to in a century.

But the real orator has almost entirely disappeared from the legal stage. The scenes have shifted. The age of forensic eloquence has gone, with all of its attendant glories and attractions. The practical, brief, crisp, utterances of the modern lawyer have succeeded. Exordiums and perorations are abolished by rules of court, which establish the limit of legal oratory, from twenty minutes, to two hours. Every oral argument must be, boiled down, to the actual bone of the contention, and the graces of rhetoric are necessarily banished. In proportion as legal oratory has been curtailed, what are called legal "briefs" have expanded. To supply that which cannot be spoken, or to instruct an ignorant, too busy, or indolent judiciary, briefs are made to an absurd length—often reaching a good-sized duodecimo, of from one to five hundred pages—leaving nothing to the imagination, or intelligence, of the judges who are to read them; mainly because the Bar is afraid to trust everything to their learning and industry.

In jury trials, professional success is attained before the addresses are made. The skill of the lawyer in handling witnesses, his capacity to twist and magnify facts, the placing of all the circumstances in a dramatic light—these are the means which tell upon the jury. The great *mise en scène* effects are what bring results.

Of course it counts to be able to "sum up" well, to group quickly the facts together, in such a way as to catch the minds of a few of the more intelligent jurors, who dominate and capture their fellow jurors in the jury room. I do not mean that wrong is perpetrated. In general, the results of jury trials are just. I say in general, for juries often go astray; but not in a greater proportion than long ago. The distinction I am trying to make clear is, that in times past the

advocates and advocacy were different. The
lawyers before the war, and the lawyers of to-day,
are as different as the steam engines of now and
then. Place an ancient and a modern locomo-
tive together, and one cannot suppress an ex-
clamation. The great criminal lawyer, David
Paul Brown, of Philadelphia, wore a swallow-
tail coat and brass buttons, a buff vest, and sympathetic trousers. Before he addressed a jury,
he carefully placed his gold snuff box in front of
him, took from his pocket a bandanna, silk hand-
kerchief, blew his nose in the true spirit of a snuff
fiend, glanced slowly and carefully around the
court room, and after many minutes of clever
preliminary acting, he bowed gravely to the
Court, and began his classic, ornate, address to
the "gentlemen of the jury."

George M. Wharton, also of the Philadelphia
bar, in another way exemplified the difference
between past and present. In looks and size he
was not unlike Napoleon. So gentle, and yet so
keen—so deep, and yet so clear; and strong,
without any rage, whether addressing a court or
jury. With a gentle and graceful gesticulation,
his voice was pitched so that every word was
heard without a loud or dissonant sound, and
the copious accents of legal knowledge flowed
from his lips and found lodgment in every listener.
No modern lawyer is apparently satisfied with

himself unless he can shout and use passionate or furious gestures. And after "a great physical" effort (as some wit has justly pronounced it) of voice and body, and not brains, he is often encouraged by an admiring client, or audience, who acclaim it "a great speech," an "eloquent presentation!" To such base uses truly have we come!

I refer to Mr. X. of New York as one of the best illustrations of the modern lawyer—neither an eloquent nor finished speaker, classical scholar, nor profound lawyer, and yet having elements of all of these; and, what is greatest, a mind pre-eminently distinguishable for its practical ability to master details, and to evoke clear business results from complicated conditions: crisp, sharp, and quick.

The judges now give an advocate hardly time to clear his throat, but brusquely inform him that he may have twenty minutes, half an hour, or an hour, as circumstances demand. To expect classic eloquence under such conditions would be altogether absurd. Alas! there are too many cases on the calendar now; too many impatient jurors; too much business; to tolerate rhetoric! Of course I do not forget the never-failing tendency of lawyers to talk *in infinitum*. It has always been necessary to check them. In all ages the habit to talk illimitably has existed. Hardly a lawyer ever believes he has said enough. Still, the modern jury lawyer makes the most of his time. He bangs away at the facts regardless of logic, order, rhetoric, or anything really oratorical; he simply hammers into his half-hour limit, in tones of thunder, or of slick and measured entreaty, or by violent denunciation or inflammatory appeals, or in a calm and seductive voice, all that he has to say. He uses just those particular weapons which will catch the jurors; and how can you blame him for not imitating David Paul Brown? Circumstances truly alter cases. Of course I am speaking of civil trials. In criminal cases there is still room for real and effective oratory. It is sometimes heard.

The truth is that the profession of the law, as a purely intellectual and classic, and, I may add, scientific pursuit, reached its zenith—its Augustan Era—at the commencement of the Civil War. It is not to be expected that lawyers should escape the influence of a war, which, as a first consequence, closed the era of pure constitutional discussion. That discussion, in its great aspects, had been kept alive by the friction between the States, and it was the most august function of the lawyer, both in the courts and the legislatures, to engage authoritatively in it. When that mode of controversy was superseded by arms, the noblest of his functions—the very head and front—were gone.

As a great scholar and lawyer wrote to me in commenting upon the difference between past and present:

> "A sense of changed conditions spread over everything. The conscience of the Nation was merged in the pride and glory of successful war. The sensitiveness as to the intellectual value of high legal attainment and effort was lost with the circumstances which had made them necessary. Then came the influx of wealth, the creation of new sources of prosperity and power, the growing sense of empire. As opposed to these, the Bar presented the spectacle of distinct bodies of men who, however deserving, had been shorn of their highest centralizing motive, who were without a local center as in England, but were split up into parts often incongruous, mere fractions of many separate communities, every day becoming more numerous."

Slowly and noiselessly as the falling tide, the change set in, until, gradually and imperceptibly, the lawyer has been deprived of most of those splendid qualities, which once made his office so illustrious in the land.

Wealth has stolen his social position; intellectual and scholastic attainments no longer win— because they are rarely found combined with a practical and adaptable mind; the cultivation of eloquence has fallen into desuetude; much of his professional occupation and emoluments have been taken from him by combinations largely composed of laymen, by "Title Searching" companies, and collection and other mere business agencies, whose principal alleged merit towards the community is cheapness; and the lawyer stands before the community shorn of his prestige, clothed in the unattractive garb of a mere commercial agent—a flexible and convenient go-between, often cultivating every kind of equivocal quality as the means of success, rather than a deep and accurate knowledge of the principles of jurisprudence—but always an exceptionally good business man.

The change in the legal profession, in the character, influence, and position of the lawyer, are more vividly illustrated in the large cities of the country. In the rural districts some traces of old professional life still exist, but even there the old guard of lawyers is succumbing to the influences which have wrought the change elsewhere, and is disappearing behind the hills of the past like a setting sun.

I do not mean to broadly assert that the calling of a lawyer has lost all of its honorableness, or that his general influence has been entirely dissipated. I affirm, however, that his aristocratic and social prestige has disappeared; that his

C

moral and intellectual standard has been lowered, and that the natural and legitimate influence, which his office entitles him to wield, no longer exists in its proper vigor. Since the war, a deep and profound gulf has been made between the past and the present; and out of the prolific womb of national life, a new legal epoch has been born; a new race of lawyers, different in education, manners, and thought from our legal ancestors, has sprung up, lacking the dignity, learning, and influence, which the old régime possessed.

CHAPTER IV.

THE PRESS, THE STAGE, THE LITERATURE, AND THE BAR, SINCE THE CIVIL WAR.

NEW epochs in national life, in the habits, manners, and morals of the people, are not ushered in to the sound of trumpets and martial music, or by written declarations or proclamations as political principles sometimes are,—like Magna Charta and the Declaration of Independence. They cannot be traced to a certain time and place, but noiselessly and gradually grow out of prevailing conditions of commercial, social, and political life,—evolution. No one can accurately fix the birth of national habits, and it is only when they are fastened upon us, like the parasite upon the tree, that we are deeply aroused to their existence.

It cannot be overlooked that the new historical era, inaugurated in this country by the Civil War, was followed by changes of the most radical nature, not only in the national characteristics, manners, and habits of the people, but in all professions, trades, and businesses, and noticeably so in the professions of law, journalism, histrionic art, and in general literature. As I have said, the organs of public opinion, like those of the body, are generally sympathetic. What affects the one, quickly communicates itself to the others.

It may at least serve the purpose of an illustration of the changes which have come over us, of the Bar, to advert to the Press, the Stage, and Literature, because a brief comparison between these last-named occupations, before and after the war, furnishes a proper analogy and prelude to a study of the condition of the legal profession.

Contrasted with those of forty years ago, the newspapers are almost unrecognizable. They are now huge, illustrated, pictorial magazines, daily chronicling all the events of the world, with more or less accuracy—running the whole gamut of human and divine affairs—entering, with fiendish glee, into the minutest details of social and domestic life, and then sold for a mere song. The reader is furnished daily with not only a full statement of the doings of the whole world, because the throbbings of the telegraph give out every minute the news from all quarters of the globe, but he has photographs of the principal actors in these occurrences,—accompanied by graphic pictures of the events,—and this huge journal is placed, in a metropolis, every morning, upon the breakfast table. The avidity for news is ravenous. It is part of our business to know whatever anybody has done, or is going to do.

The editorial has given way to the news column. The genius and talents of the newspaper writers, however, have by no means vanished. Impromptu productions frequently appear, in the daily and weekly press, which are strikingly brilliant and clever, and which will not unfavorably compare, as mere writings, with the choicest morsels of the best classic writers. Wit and humor also abound in the press, inimitable and illimitable, if not always Attic. Advertisements are seduced from the shopkeepers and business community by a large circulation, and the large circulation is gained by portraying, in sensational colors, every event calculated to attract the notice, tickle the humor or fancies, or arouse the passions, of the masses. The central aim of the newspaper proprietor, however, is to make money, through the advertisement columns, and the real purpose of journalism, alas, becomes subordinated to the greed of the age—"put money in thy purse." The personality of the newspaper owner never appears. His genius is reflected in the advertising columns.

The most striking feature of the modern newspaper is its diversified occupation. Its function is no longer simply confined to printing news and animadverting upon public questions—it is no longer a guide and a teacher. A newspaper is now an institution—the head of which is a "business manager." It promotes all kinds of charities, eleemosynary and other public works—it gives and collects vast sums of money for these purposes—it awards prizes—it establishes national landmarks—it is an intelligence office and detective bureau. The journals outvie with each other in their advocacy, and financial support, of philanthropic measures. They furnish the sick and fever-heated needy with ice, and the hungry with soup; they establish summer and winter homes for the poor, and perform manifold deeds of genuine benevolence. They hunt down criminals and boldly usurp every duty of the district attorney, magistrate, and policeman, and espouse the rights of the public in the civil courts of justice. A newspaper as thus conducted is a bureau, not a journal!—a self-established, self-supporting newspaper, literary, political, sporting, and miscellaneous bureau!—put in motion by individuals to make money, and often to advance personal and political interests.

It must be admitted, however, that in their manifold undertakings the newspapers are not always inspired by the true spirit of charity or justice. The right hand not only knoweth what the left hand doeth, but the whole body is advised thereof, and the plans and details are blazoned out, and "trumpet tongued" to the world. They make lavish and ostentatious gifts, and in this and a thousand other ways abuse their power by hounding the public into doing likewise—or seduce contributions from them by tickling their vanity, and parading the names of the donors in conspicuous parts of the paper. Individual security, if not often directly invaded, is still felt to be held by a kind of sufferance. And the privacy and sacredness of domestic life! It is an open book; I need not speak of it. An immense capital is now required to conduct one of these metropolitan bureaus, and no matter how brilliant, talented, and eloquent a writer may be, without great financial resources, it is practically impossible for him to establish and maintain a newspaper.

The effect of the change in journalism, of its departure from the real and noble purposes of the Press, has been, gradually, to weaken its influence with the people upon many public questions. Its opinions and conclusions are becoming gradually less effective, its utterances are looked upon with amusement or suspicion; its wails and shrieks, and death-like headlines, have become so frequent, that they are fatiguing. The readers, satiated with sensationalism, treat the recommendations of the journals with a feeling akin to contempt. It is natural that when a community discovers that newspapers discuss public questions for the pure pecuniary benefit of their owners, they must lose all moral force as leaders or teachers of public thought. In a word, the newspapers are transformed into advertising bureaus. The aim of the proprietor is to catch the advertisers—that of the advertisers is to catch the public.

The "theatrical world" also discloses radical changes. The stage, in its pristine condition, should be one of the most powerful organs of public opinion. In its proper sphere, it holds up to approbation the lives and acts of virtue, and directly or indirectly, through the terrible weapons of ridicule, satire, or wit, condemns vice and maintains the supremacy of the law. The new drama is almost entirely realistic and sensational. There are many exceptions, of course, but even they have not wholly escaped from the prevailing influence. The ability, genius, talent, of the actors, exist, but an apprentice to the stage who wished to make money—to be popular—would hardly neglect to cultivate dancing and singing as principal accomplishments for his profession. And who goes to the theater to study pure English? In the main, and as the rule, literature and poetry, the chief glories of the drama, have been entirely divorced from it. In going to a theater, the best we can hope to see is some admirably arranged spectacular effect, which is expected to compensate for any poverty of higher attributes in the actor or the author. The actor has hardly a distinctive chance to shine. Shakespeare cannot any longer stand on his own unaided merits; he must be tricked out with the appliances of modern "art" before he can be made to "draw." Descending lower, we have something in comparison with which the rudest Thespian buffoonery of the ancient time was respectable and interesting. Need it be specified? Acrobatic feats, trivial puns, vulgar witticisms, and a senseless display of tumbling, tossing, and shuffling upon the stage—tragedy, comedy, and vaudeville, all hopelessly mingled together—which tend to convert the actors into clowns. The sensual and material tendencies of the age are nowhere more strikingly illustrated than on the stage. But the theatrical manager knows the public taste. He must "hit" that taste between wind and water. And the beautiful, majestic, ennobling thoughts of a dramatic author, filled with an ambition to do something real for his age, are frequently consigned to the flames, or the waste-paper basket.

Lastly, comes general literature, *belles-lettres*, closely following prevailing fashions and habits.

Myriads of books and periodicals are yearly turned out upon the world, covering almost every conceivable theme of human thought. The great, leading characteristics of these productions is the effort to say something new, or to say it in such a way that it may appear to be new. It is one of the wonders of the age to see how many men and women have devoted themselves to writing books. It is no longer a question of learning, but one of "knack," to be an author. When Madame Leo Hunter gave her fête champêtre, Dickens recounts with inimitable humor, that there were congregated in an acre lot, nearly all of the authors of the day. To see *one* author in those days was a sight to be remembered; but Pickwick had the felicity to mingle with, and talk to, all of them in a morning—all *real* authors!

History, geography, and science are ransacked to furnish material which, tortured into a thousand shapes, may yield the requisite attraction to insure notoriety and profit. We may admire the ingenuity displayed in all this, but does the merit of it rise higher? The solid basis of a classic taste, judgment tempering into sobriety, expression, and invention, the desire to improve (a kind of religion in the mind of the writer) by adding something genuine to the scope of human sympathy and knowledge, are now only incidental and very rare. The whole character of that species of writing which so largely influences the mental habitudes may be roughly summed up by the word "sensational"; but it has many degrees and many shades and is by no means confined to mere purely imaginative productions. It affects the Pulpit, and, as we have shown, the Press; it even invades the scientific. The public yields to the fascination, and, while they toss the books aside, carry the tastes they form, and the standards they impress, abroad with them into thought and action. The few who cherish better models are so much at a discount that ordinarily they shrink from obtruding them, fearing a controversy in which they cannot convince, and can only feel themselves degraded.

A singular evidence of the decline of the true æsthetic faculty is the little encouragement given to Poetry of the highest order; yet it is certain that without great poetry there can be no great literature. Much poetry has undoubtedly been written in these days, and much of it is good; but it has ceased to be a thing which men take to their "business and bosoms."

A practical thought, in view of the multiplicity of these productions, is the extremely low price of paper, and the improvement in the art of typesetting machinery, which enable newspapers and books to be published, at a price, fabulously low.

If the price of paper were raised to ten cents a pound, one-half of the world of literature would disappear in the abyss of time, modern literature would receive a deadly blow—and shall I say, the people an untold blessing? And what is the responsibility of the publishers for this condition? The classic publishers! who dote upon the best models of English literature! The same remark applies to them as to the theatrical managers, and the owners of newspapers. They feed the public with the food they relish—and give them plenty for their money.

The moral sense—the conscience of a nation—is exposed through public opinion. The barometers which reveal the moral, social, political, and intellectual condition of a people, are the great organs of which I have spoken.

As they are, so are the people. These organs are their faithful representatives. They change with the habits and thoughts of the people. In these days they rarely lead and make public opinions,—they oftener follow it. They are usually reflective and not creative forces. There is very little see-sawing between the Press, Stage, and Literature, and the People. They are generally upon an even keel. If public conscience is healthy, the Pulpit, Press, and Stage are likely to be healthy; if it is abnormal or diseased, they are apt to be demoralized or sick.

Critics who assume to rise above the surface of things, are constantly saying: "Look at the Press —how low and degraded." "Behold the depraved condition of the Stage." "The Bar, intellectually and morally, is not what it was once." "Even the Pulpit is demoralized."

But such critics are simply inviting the people to look at themselves. These great organs generally hold up a faithful mirror of prevailing culture, tastes, fashions, morals, and habits. They are too clever and skillful to be out of tune with public conscience and taste. They give the people exactly what they demand. They are low and coarse, and unfaithful to their true missions, only when the people require them to be so.

Returning to the law. It would seem quite unnatural, if striking changes should not have crept into that profession. It was as quick, as the other organs of public opinion, to adapt itself to the demands of new conditions.

One of the first changes, in the practice of the law, was created inside of the profession itself. More than thirty years ago, a few lawyers organized a company, to search or investigate titles, and facilitate the transfers of real estate, for a fee incomparably lower than that charged by a considerable body of the profession, who were known as "Conveyancers." Later, other companies were formed, until the entire business relating to titles, and transfers of real estate, has passed from the hands of individual lawyers into these companies. Title companies were incorporated to examine the titles to real estate, and other companies to manage decedent and trust estates; agencies were organized to collect all kinds of mercantile accounts, and other combinations were formed to do general legal business.

These corporations, or combinations, these legal "trusts," created to transact, by wholesale, all kinds of law business, formerly performed by individual members of the Bar, have at length absorbed a very large share of the lawyer's former work, and gradually driven him into other fields of employment. The characteristics of the lawyers changed, with the change in their occupation. From "Attorneys and Counselors at Law" they became agents, solicitors, practical promoters, and commercial operators. They attached themselves to all kinds of corporations, as officers and directors. Entering the offices of some of the law firms in a metropolitan city, one imagines that he is in a commercial counting-room, or banking department. Nothing can better illustrate the change of the profession. Most of the intellectual and professional glamour of the Bar has flown, and law has become a business. It is the boast of some legal firms that their mere office expenses run over fifty thousand dollars a year. The "outdoor" or office business of the lawyer has become the most profitable; and colossal fees, as commissions, are often paid to them, upon the successful close of financial and business operations, in which no litigation is involved. A vast contingent business has been inaugurated. One lawyer received more than a million of dollars as a contingent reward; and a fee of one hundred thousand dollars is no longer regarded with astonishment. In many transactions the lawyers are half bankers and half lawyers. Of course, the inevitable effect of these employments, is to remove the lawyer far away from his technical and intellectual pursuits, to change his habits, and to cause him to forget, or neglect, the true mission of his profession.

Thousands of lawyers seek livelihood and prominence in political life, and the offices cannot be created fast enough for them to fill. Some enter politics to advertise themselves; others because they cannot gain a livelihood in any other manner.

Political, social, and business associations are often more cultivated, by the young lawyers, than a knowledge of jurisprudence. Through the door of politics most American lawyers reach the Bench. The fact constitutes, perhaps, one of the most demoralizing influences of the age. It is known, talked of, criticised and yet tolerated, if not sanctioned, by the voters. Vehement protests are from time to time made against it, but in vain.

The people do not seem to comprehend the

seriousness of the practice, or if they do they are indifferent. In general the best equipped lawyer, in character and learning, has no more chance to become a judge, without political influences, than he has to turn water into wine. The people are the eventual sufferers, because while some good men are chosen, the majority have not the necessary accomplishments, or a proper conception of their duties. Law then becomes more or less a chance, and delays and other manifest evils supervene, for all of which the people eventually suffer. Its demoralizing influence upon the bar is indescribable. It lowers the respect which lawyers should have for the judges. It removes all incentive to study and real ambition. But beyond all of these things, it shows that the combined influence of the bar, is not strong enough, to correct an evil which destroys its own prestige and morale. Lawyers become schemers and office-seekers. They neither demand, nor care for, the approbation of their brethren of the bar. The qualities of audacity and immodesty, supplant those of learning and fitness. The man with real accomplishments, refuses to enter into a contest for the judgeship, and the race is narrowed down to those who are willing to proclaim most loudly, their own merits, and spend their time in pulling the party ropes.

If a lawyer can obtain judicial position, by

attaching himself to a political organization, why should he take the more rugged, trying, and uncertain path to professional glory by hard and laborious legal study and cultivation? If the lawyer can obtain clients by becoming a member of a social, or political club, or church, of a civic, or eleemosynary association, why should he weary his brain and mental faculties with profound or steady intellectual occupation?

If he can obtain references, receiverships, and patronage by cultivating the Judges, instead of tying himself to books, why should he not become the inseparable companion of some friendly Judge?

I am endeavoring to show what a lawyer is to-day. The difference between what he is, and what he should be, is as wide as the ocean. What he should be, is the never to be realized *ideal;* what he is —the always existing *actual.* We must study both. Keeping them in open juxtaposition is the only real means to advancement and reform.

In the selection of judges, I believe the evils could be largely reduced by holding separate elections for the Judiciary. The question of the fitness and character of each candidate could then be, independently, examined. As it is now, the elections are general, and the merits of judicial nominees are lost sight of under, what are regarded as, more important issues.

D

CHAPTER V.

To judge of the quality of our lawyers, to use
a commercial phrase, it is necessary to know of
what, and how, they are made; to know the
course of studies they pursue before they are
admitted to practice. As the lawyer is trained,
so he grows. To produce lawyers who can perform their duties, they should be taught to cultivate a moral sense; the nature and object of law;
the nature and duties of citizenship; the nature
and duties of a legislator; but above and beyond
everything else, they should be taught the real
mission of the lawyer—which includes professional ethics. These fundamental requisites to
the making of a full lawyer are almost entirely
overlooked in all of the courses of education
followed in law offices, law schools, and academies or colleges. Lawyers are made up to be
mere instruments for their clients, without any

50

attention being paid to their duties to the State. The fact is extraordinary, nay, incredible. But it is true. One cannot blame the professors. The curriculum of legal study is based upon codification. I mean the sentiment of codification, pervades and influences all legal education. A candidate, through the ordinary course of preliminary legal study, knows nothing of moral philosophy, professional ethics, or the mission of a lawyer. Neither Paley, Austin, Savigny, Kant, Domat, Burlamaqui, Montesquieu, Pothier —nor even Blackstone—except in a fragmentary manner—or any other book or course of studies calculated to impart the above fundamental knowledge—is studied as part of the curriculum, and rarely at all.[1]

"To the student who begins the study of English Law, without some previous knowledge of the rationale of law, in general, it naturally appears an assemblage of arbitrary and unconnected rules. But if he approached it with a well-grounded knowledge, of the general principles of jurisprudence, and with a map of a body of law distinctly impressed upon his mind, he might obtain a clear conception of it, as a system, or organic whole, with comparative ease and rapidity." [2]

[1] See in this connection Chapter X, where remedies are discussed.

[2] Austin's Lectures, III 362.

In like manner, Mr. Phillips in his able and independent discussion of Jurisprudence says:[1]

> "I firmly believe that the intolerable aridity, usually attributed to legal study, is entirely due to the infatuation with which the student usually persists in exploring the details of his science, before he comprehends its outlines. What every jurist has first to do, is to make himself master, not of the law itself, which may be pernicious and must be imperfect, but of that great system of jural problems which forms the framework of all law, and which, as it arises out of the conditions of human existence, must retain its importance while the human race survives. Let him once clearly perceive how these questions have become necessary and how they are connected with each other, and he will have little difficulty in understanding and criticising the various solutions of which they are capable. Let him once thoroughly comprehend what is *to be done*, and the inquiry how it *has been* done will become an easy one."

Let one more quotation, embodying the authority of Prof. Sheldon Amos, describe, in his own vigorous and graphic language, the general perplexity and confusion of the young student of English law arising from the lack of clear scientific guidance:

[1] Phillips' Jurisprudence, 26, 27.

"It cannot be surprising," he says, "if the young English student approaches the Science of Jurisprudence with somewhat of a quivering heart and trembling gait. He knows not where he is going, and is not quite sure whether he is going, or wanting to go, anywhere. He thirsts for something broader, deeper, more indestructible than anything he can find in Text Books of English Law, or in the successive modifications in the substance of law itself.

"He hears of 'Jurisprudence' and he has a dim hope, that what he is in search of, may perchance be there. He draws near, and in place of a science, or a systematic exhibition of what is universal and everlasting, he is often enough regaled with nothing more satisfactory than a story of incessant change, the dreary register of meaningless variety, the loose guesses of politicians and moralists, the reckless verbiage of those who have studied just law enough to confuse the spontaneous workings of their conscience, and yet who affect just sensitiveness enough of conscience to interfere with their unflinching interpretation of a single law." [1]

A candidate for the Bar must, before admission,

[1] Systematic View of the Science of Jurisprudence, page 508. I am glad to say, however, that in the course of instruction of the Columbian University lectures upon the "Elements of Law," "Modern Civil Law," and the "History of European Law" are given by a very competent person, Professor Munroe Smith. But it is subordinate and collateral, and for want of time inadequately appreciated.

be a citizen of the State in which he applies to practice, and of the United States. He must be of legal age, and possess certain moral and educational qualifications, which are the *sine qua non* to admission everywhere. Moral character means, as intimated, an ability to show, by a certificate from third persons, that the candidate is a fit person to be admitted to the Bar. A man may have a good character, and yet know nothing of the ethics and mission of the profession. The general educational qualifications are ordinary. A smattering of history, geography, grammar, and Latin.

Besides these requisites, the applicant must pass an examination before an examining board of lawyers, or, in some States, produce a certificate from a law school or college.

Considering the relation which lawyers bear to this Government, and the American people, the examination for admission to the Bar, is superficial. The applicant is only required to have been an apprentice, for two or three years. It is unnecessary, at this time, to criticise in detail the curriculum.[1] Let it suffice that it is entirely inadequate to produce a lawyer. The student attends a course of lectures; skims through a few legal works; is subjected to desultory examinations; crams himself for a final "quiz"

[1] See Post, Chap. X.

before the Examiners of the Court; and he is a lawyer, and generally, moreover, without having been under the care or tutelage of an active practitioner. Modern methods of legal education are akin to the age. Lawyers are machine made. By a patented process, one can put a log of wood in a machine, and it comes out a box of matches. The aim of law schools and colleges is to manufacture the lawyers quickly. Hardly any of the instructors or professors have any practical knowledge of the profession. They are theorists and students. They have no clinical experience. They know almost nothing of the real office, and mission of the lawyer. They are intelligent enough—many of them savants—and remarkably bright men, withal; but each of them has a large class of students on his hands, and the sole aim is to carry it safely through the final examination, and lawyers are manufactured *en bloc*. When they first see the light of the professional world, like new-born babes, they look around in astonishment, and wonder why they are brought into professional life so feebly equipped.

Young lawyers, therefore, start out in their professional journey with a keen sense of their own incompetency. The preliminary education which they have received does not carry them beyond the point of their examination, and when they embark into actual professional work, they have little—certainly no adequate—idea of the functions, powers, and duties of the office, which they have been licensed to hold.

The student must first obtain a license from the court. No duly certified applicant can practice the profession of law without such a license, based upon an oath, hereafter referred to. This at once gives the lawyer an official position, in his relation to the court and the community.

While any person may set himself up as a carpenter, tailor, baker, agent, banker, or broker, or pursue any other legal occupation (except that of medicine, where a certificate, for obvious reasons, is necessary), in any place, and on whatever scale, he desires,[1] the policy of the law, as evidenced first by rules of the court, and afterwards by statute, has at all times been to place limited restrictions upon admissions to the Bar.

[1] This was not always the law, for anciently, as will be seen by the Statute which I quote, all persons practicing any occupation were required to serve an apprenticeship. Stat. 5, Eliz., Chap. 4 (1562–63), Sec. XXIV, is as follows:

"And be it further enacted by the authoritie aforesaid, that after the first daye of Maie next coming, it shall not bee lawful for any pson or psons, other than such as doo now lawfully use or exercise any Arte Misterye or Manuell Occupacon, to set uppe occupie use or exercise anye Crafte Misterye or Occupacon, nowe used or occupied within the Realm of Englande or Wales, Except he shall have been brought uppe therein Seaven Yeares at the least as Apprentice, in maner and fourme aforesaid, nor to set anye person or woorck in suche Misterye Arte or Occupacon, being not a worchman at this daye except he shall have been Apprentice as ys aforesaid, orels having served as an Apprentice as ys

Litigants and suitors, who might otherwise justly complain, are authorized to represent themselves, and to advocate their own causes— a privilege of which, with marked good sense, they rarely avail themselves.

The profession of the lawyer, therefore, stands out distinctly and separately distinguished from other trades and occupations. He starts on his professional career marked as an official—an officer of the court.

The origin of this is clear, and the reason for it is as strong to-day as when the office was first created, viz: the lawyer was regarded as the friend, the adviser, the associate, of the court, and he became, as he is now styled (but for different purposes than those for which the distinction was first applied to him), "an officer of the court," acting under the supervision and control of the latter. The courts accordingly mark out the qualifications of these officials—their own officers.

In these days, when a lawyer is styled "an officer of the court," it is generally in connection with some effort to punish him for a dereliction of duty, and this term is rarely, if ever, used in its original and just sense, viz: to signify that he

aforesaid, shall or will become a Journeyman, or bee hired by the Yere; upon payne that willingly offending or dooing the contrary shall forfeit and lose for every default fourtye Shillinges for every monethe."

is an officer to advise, aid, and assist the court in the administration of justice. Indeed, the tendency of the courts everywhere is not to regard the lawyer as an arm of the court, so much as to hold him at arm's length—to treat him as one ready and willing to accept, if not actually seeking, rights to which he is not entitled, the effect of which, upon the manners, culture, and *esprit de corps* of the profession, can be readily imagined. Still, the lawyers are officers of the court. They may be said to always rest under the command of the court. Undoubtedly they can always be called upon to assist and aid the court.

Another feature of the subject is, that no restrictions are placed upon the number of lawyers who may practice the profession.

So far as any demonstrated policy is concerned, the public seems to be indifferent whether there are five, or five hundred, or five hundred thousand lawyers, in existence. This liberality has been bountifully appreciated. The lawyers have increased to such proportion, in every community, that the profession is full to repletion. Still, they are not any more numerous than they were at one time in Naples. Addison is authority for a story that when Innocent the Eleventh desired the Marquis of Carpio, to furnish him with 30,000 head of swine, the Marquis answered him that for his swine he could not spare them, but if his

Holiness had occasion for 30,000 lawyers, he had them at his service.[1] The Marquis must have had a large estate!

Of course, the effect of turning out hordes of legal incompetents, is as bad for the latter, as for society. They both suffer. Hundreds of lawyers, finding nothing to do, in a few years seek other employments; many of them eke out a meager and starving existence by filling clerk-ships, and other subordinate positions, with their more fortunate brethren; still others, lacking the ability, or knowledge, to perform the work intrusted to them, turn their professional labors into a regular business and merchandise system, by associations or partnerships, and various other kinds of occupations. The enormous increase in the number of corporations has been an unlimited blessing to a certain class of lawyers. These corporations have, through the influence of nepotism, furnished a delightful haven to many a lawyer, otherwise unequipped, with natural, educational, or practical ability. The fact that social or political influence, could secure him a snug berth, in a corporate position, has frequently been the sole incentive to his adoption of the legal profession.

No statistics, I believe, have ever been made, or suppositions drawn, as to the number of law-

[1] "Remarks on Italy," Vol. 2, p. 429.

yers necessarily required to transact the business of the country; but it is generally agreed that there are now vastly too many for such service; that, in the language of political economy, the supply very largely exceeds the demand.

No limit should, or perhaps could, ever be placed upon the number of lawyers entitled to practice, except by ordaining such rigid preliminary studies and qualifications as would act as a deterrent. If candidates enrolling as legal apprentices were fully convinced that to become a lawyer meant serious study and application, there would be fewer candidates. As long as a course of study exists, which offers inducements for individuals to become members of the Bar, with a mere smattering of intellectual training, the profession will be filled to repletion. There are other concurring causes, of course. Young ambition, the pride and vanity of parents and friends, mistaken notions of the true nature of the profession, all go to swell the ranks, so that the gates are thrown wide open, and access made easy, to the very class who are least qualified, when they have passed through to admission, to encounter the steep and stony paths that lead to genuine success. My purpose at present is only to draw attention to the effect of all this on the community. As to its personal effect upon the lives and fortunes of the aspirants, another book might be written. It is enough to say that no miseries are greater than those which follow the mistaken choice of a profession.

The census shows that in 1850 there were 23,939 practicing lawyers in the United States; and the table compiled from the same source shows the following result in ensuing decades:

Year	Total Population	Total Number of Lawyers	Approximate Proportion of Lawyers to Population
1850	23,191,876	23,939	Say 1 to 1,000
1860	31,443,321	33,193	1 to 950
1870	38,558,371	40,736	1 to 945
1880	50,155,783	64,137	1 to 780
1890	62,622,250	89,630	1 to 687
1900	76,303,387	114,703	1 to 665

If the ratio keeps running as this table shows, anyone can estimate the time, when there will be a lawyer for each one hundred inhabitants. It will be quite necessary, if the laws and decisions accumulate with the same rapidity as they now do.

The lawyer is launched into the community without any compass to denote the course of his professional career. He has a brevet to follow any, or all, of the branches of jurisprudence, real estate, commercial, maritime, patent, and criminal law. If his tastes and inclination permit, he may also engage in any secular business, or undertaking—either separately, or in conjunction with his law practice—a privilege very frequently availed of, but I think to the discredit of the profession.

The sphere of the lawyer's operations is limited, or confined, to the State in which he is admitted, and to the Federal Courts, if he be admitted therein; although, as a matter of comity, he frequently appears in courts outside of his own State.

In the present inflated and complicated condition of the law, it goes by the mere saying, that any lawyer who has simply passed through the formal system of study prescribed, and who has been licensed to practice, cannot be presumed to comprehend any of the principal branches of the law. At best, he only acquires a smattering of some of them.

It may be said on the other side, that nobody is injured by this ignorance, because litigants do not, as a rule, employ young lawyers, who fight and struggle along many years before they attain the full confidence of clients. But, as I shall show, the lawyer's duties to the government are of equal, if not of greater, importance than those which he owes his clients, and to turn upon the community hordes of incompetent practitioners lowers the standard of the profession, deprives the Bar of the learning and respect which are so necessary to enable it to defend and exercise its proper position, and nullifies the influence which it naturally possesses in private and public affairs.

Great talent and strong bias, towards the profession, in the individual may overcome all difficulties, but these, with their results, can be equally shown by the work accomplished previous to examination. A professional morale in the student, meeting with the same quality in those who are delegated to examine, is quickly ascertained and understood; but where the tendency of the whole system is to produce a class of incompetents, applicants and examining boards standing on exactly the same level, the results become obvious; with such an initiative, it is vain to say that the evil corrects itself; that the student's real education begins after admission. The profession and the community alike (indeed, in this respect they may be considered one and the same interest) are entitled to some better guarantee.

The oath which the lawyer takes before entering upon his official career is slightly different in each of the States. This oath throws some light upon the lawyer's real functions and duties. The forms which are given below practically illustrate those of all of the States, and of England and France.

UNITED STATES SUPREME COURT.

I, ————, do solemnly swear (or affirm, as the case may be) that I will demean myself, as an attorney and counselor of this Court, *uprightly and according to law;* and that I will support the Constitution of the United States.

NEW YORK.

I, ————, do solemnly swear (or affirm, as the case may be) that I will support the Constitution of the United States and the Constitution of the State of New York; and that I will faithfully *discharge the duties* of the *office* of attorney and counselor-at-law, according to the best of my ability.

PENNSYLVANIA.

You do swear (or affirm) that you will support the Constitution of the United States and the Constitution of this Commonwealth, and that you will behave yourself in the office of Attorney within this Court, according to the best of your learning and ability, and with all good fidelity, as well to the Court as to *the client ;* that you will *use no falsehood, nor delay any person's cause for lucre or malice.*

ENGLAND.

I, ————, do swear that I will truly and honestly demean myself in the practice of a Solicitor according to the best of my knowledge and ability, so help me God!

FRANCE.

In France, the Advocate's oath of office requires him "de refuser les causes dont il connaitrait l'iniquite." [1]

By the ancient laws of Scotland, it was required that "advocates on the time of their admission, and yearly, should be sworn to execute their office of advocation diligently and truly; and that as soon as they understood their client's cause to be unjust or wrongful, they should incontinently leave the same and desist from all further pursuit and defense." [2] And the law of Spain imposed upon them an oath that "they will conduct themselves faithfully and will not defend unjust causes." [3]

The oath which he takes before the Supreme Court, of the United States, binds him only to do that which in conscience and law he is compelled to do as a good citizen, viz.: to "demean myself uprightly and according to law;" that of New York, to "discharge the duties of the *office* of Attorney and Counselor-at-Law, according to

[1] "Usages et Regles de la Profession d'Avocat," etc., par M. Cresson, Vol. I, p. 17.

[2] Statutes of the Lords, 13th June, 1537.

[3] "Institutes of the Civil Law of Spain," cited in O'Brien's Lawyers.

E

the best of my ability," is equally vague, because
the duties are not defined; that of Pennsylvania,
"with all good fidelity, as well to the Court as to
the Client; that you will use no *falsehood*, nor
delay any person's *cause* for *lucre or malice*,"
throws a little more light upon the lawyer's
duties, and upon the opportunities he has to
use, disloyally and dishonestly, his office. The
Advocates' oath in France, to refuse cases *which
he knows to be wrong*, still further opens up the
subject.

But none of these formal oaths define the duties
of the lawyer; they neither explain his relations
to the court which licenses him, nor to his client,
nor to the community. All of these matters
are left to the imagination; and the young lawyers, when they are turned upon the community,
must search elsewhere than in these oaths, to
discover the full measure of their duties.

While it is true that the courts, in the exercise
of their undoubted jurisdiction over lawyers,
can, and do, punish them for such flagrant acts
as, according to the customs, tastes, perceptions,
morals, and manners of the age, constitute dishonest or disloyal acts; yet, there is no code of
ethics, or rules, prepared which opens the subject
of the lawyer's manifold duties, and teaches him
the importance of the office he fills.

Everything is now left to the moral perception

of the lawyers, and the conscience of the courts; and they are both groping in a wild and illimitable field of discretion, and necessarily of doubt.[1]

[1] I note with satisfaction that the American Bar Association has taken up the subject of professional ethics. Its agitation ought to awaken introspection; but its effect must be, necessarily, superficial. Ethics must be taught to the students as part of their preliminary education.

CHAPTER VI.

NATURE OF LAWYER'S VOCATION.

THE lawyer is called "an officer of the Court;" but, as I have said, before, that term is, generally, applied to him in modern times, when the Courts wish, summarily, to reprimand, degrade, or punish him. The lawyer must be an "officer" to justify summary measures against him, by the Courts; otherwise it would be necessary to proceed against him by the regular course of judicial procedure, as other persons are proceeded against —in civil cases by summons; in criminal offenses by indictment. Originally, the courts called upon their brethren of the bar to advise them. In moments of need or doubt, the lawyer became of great importance to the Judges. But I repeat, in this connection, the courts have long since ceased to regard him as a real, disinterested friend, adviser and judicial adjunct. The lawyers and the courts have been effectually divorced. Still, the courts could, at any time, restore his prestige, and take him, as it were, again to their bosom, as a real official friend.

While, as a supernumerary of the court, the lawyer's vocation has been enfeebled, if not totally destroyed, apart from this fact, he is an officer of very great authority and power.

At the instance of a client, he becomes the official author and creator of all judicial proceedings. He is the fountain head from whose source all legal processes flow.

The lawyer's mandate—the summons, writ, or by whatever name the original process may be called, commands the appearance in court of the highest or lowliest individual in the land. In New York the lawyer issues the original mandate. His name, signed to a summons, is the beginning of legal proceedings.

Apart from suitors themselves—who are permitted to appear in their own cases—no judicial action can be put in motion without the sanction of some lawyer. He is the sole officer authorized to cause a civil action to be begun. If the lawyer approves the client's demand, he can issue, or cause to be issued, process which will bring into court the proudest millionaire, the most powerful magnate, or the most influential citizen or corporation. The demand may be unfounded, the action unjustified, the whole proceeding utterly without merit, in law, or in fact, yet the defendant must obey. A lawyer, the day after he is admitted, the veriest tyro in the profession may, without a tittle of justice or right, summon the worthiest and purest individual to answer the demands of a professional blackmailer; and although after years, it may be, of litigation, in which character, property, and expense are involved, the suit is dismissed as unfounded, yet the lawyer sits, serenely, in his office, secure from liability, exempted from acts which often, through his negligence or design, have caused untold mischief and damage. His ordinary mistakes of law, or judgment, cannot be made the basis of a legal demand against him. How many of such mistakes are made; how many causeless actions are instituted, can be, easily, computed by consulting the records of the Courts—which show the number of suits finally dismissed.

An individual who possesses powers like those which I have described, is forsooth, an "officer," and one whose authority is hardly exceeded by that of any other official, known to any system of government. Upon the *ipse dixit*, or judgment of the lawyer, all suits are begun or defended.

Inquiring into the origin of the lawyer's power, we find that it arises from the necessities of political organization.

The law is not automatic, or self-acting; it rests dormant until some one sets its machinery in motion. A good definition of Law, in the abstract, is that given by Hooker,—"that which doth moderate the force and power, that which doth appoint the form and measure of working, the same we term a Law . . . the very being of God is a Law to his working." In the concrete, as applied to political existence, it consists of declarations, enunciated by the supreme power of the State, of certain principles, or rules, for human government. It says to its subjects (as Blackstone puts it), "thou shalt or thou shalt not do this or that thing." These rules may be, and often are, violated both by individuals and communities, but until somebody complains, a law is a mere *brutum fulmen*. Murder goes unpunished if it is concealed; theft escapes notice if no prosecutor appears; and manifold civil rights are invaded where the party injured seeks no redress from the courts.

Now, the official and authorized agents, who put in motion the machinery of the law, are the lawyers.

When we ascertain the reason and philosophy of the subject, we begin to appreciate the full scope of the lawyer's powers.

The law is naturally separated into two great systems,—the criminal and the civil.

When a crime is committed, it is regarded as an act aimed at the entire community, and so soon as its existence is known, sworn officials, such as policemen, constables, magistrates, sheriffs, coroners, and district attorneys, start the wheels of justice which bring the offender to punishment. A crime inflicts a blow upon the autonomy of the State. It strikes at the whole people.

But when a civil injury is inflicted upon person or property, the lawyers intervene and set the machinery of the law in motion.

The "machinery of the law," does not only mean the commencement of a suit, by the service of process upon the delinquent, or offender—it means all of the steps in the litigation—what are known as the "orderly parts of a suit"—the different stages, which litigants pass through, before a final judicial settlement of their rights is reached, viz: the summons which brings the parties before the court; the complaint, or declaration, the answer or plea, the issue, the trial, the judgment, the appeal, the execution, and all of the multiplicity of interlocutory and intervening orders and proceedings, which are met with in ordinary legal and equitable actions.

Wherever justice is administered, these orderly parts of a suit,—this machinery of the law—must exist. There always must be a complainant and a defendant, a complaint and an answer, a hearing and a decision, a judgment and execution.

Even in a barbaric state, these forms are followed, though in a primitive and summary way.

The orderly parts of a suit, therefore, are coeval with the administration of justice.

In a civilized community these forms are nicely and delicately adjusted to each other, so that they operate harmoniously together, and they are designed and intended to produce as a whole, exact justice between litigants, if the machinery is properly and regularly run.

Hence these orderly steps in a suit, are necessary and substantial parts of practical jurisprudence, and although they are called the "forms" of the law, they are absolutely essential to the correct determination of legal controversies, and without them, the law simply would be a bundle of abstract principles, declaring rules for human conduct, and directing their observance, but without the necessary appendages for enforcing them, unless by a relapse to methods purely arbitrary. Without the ability to give an adequate remedy to the parties injured, after a fair hearing, the law would be nothing but a series of insipid declarations.

Now, every motion of the wheels of form, which run after they are set in motion, is regulated and watched by the lawyers. They study all of the intricate and delicate mechanism, they arrange the movements, fast or slow, and, like skillful workmen, they learn to direct, and control, the whole course of the law. The legal fencing, which is had under a Code, between the institution of a suit and a Judgment, is amazing, when one remembers that Courts exist to render speedy and exact justice. The clients disappear, and the lawyers come to the front, with their motions and counter motions, until the real controversy is lost sight of, in a cloud of technical sparring and conflicts.

The foregoing suggestions introduce the lawyer in his first great official relation to the community—standing between the Subject and the Law. I use the word "Subject" advisedly, as exactly describing the citizen, in his relation to the Law; however much it may be the work of his own creation.

Upon the lawyer's advice and judgment, the law is put in motion.

He is primarily charged to determine, in advance, whether his client has a just claim or defense. He is a kind of judge—preliminarily inquiring into his client's rights and duties.

The moral responsibility of the lawyer becomes, therefore, very great, and his office assumes an importance which superficial inquiry would not ascribe to it. Directly the machinery is set in motion by the lawyer, the suit becomes one of public concern, no matter how small or great the amount, or principle, involved. A judge, or jury, eventually appears; all the forms of the law are involved in the settlement, and the public are taxed for the general expenses of the courts. ·The importance of the whole subject to the lay community is apparent from this purely material aspect of it.

In the commencement of suits, the lawyer has need, therefore, of honesty, learning, prudence, and patriotism. It rests with him to preserve the purity of the legal system; to separate the chaff of fraud, exaggeration and doubt, from the wheat of fact and truth. For, if from ignorance, dishonesty, or indifference, to the effects of his action, he advises the commencement of an unjust suit, or the evasion or denial of a legal claim, he defeats the objects of the law, he prostitutes its forms, and brings its administration into contempt and disrepute. He poisons the fountain of justice at its source, and the evil effects are felt all through the body of the law.

Client and counsel become involved in a common atmosphere of suspicion, and a greater or less degree of moral reprobation attaches to their actions. In the ordinary judgments of men, it is the law and lawyers that suffer most; to the latter it brings a shallow reputation for cleverness, largely and sincerely blended with contempt; to the former, a sense of its inadequacy to fulfill its ordained purposes. Law is "humbug"—a mere game of chicane; the lawyer a cunning scamp, not essentially different from other scamps, except that he is better protected, and more to be feared.

Sheltered in the garb of his office, the lawyer can always, insidiously and secretly, deflect the course of justice, and defraud the law. It is hard to detect him; he is representing another's interest, and is not responsible for his client's morals or frauds. And both public policy, and express statute, prohibit him from uttering one word, passed in professional counsel.

The pleas, the defenses, the pretenses of the client, are frequently the lawyer's own work, but they are made in the name of the client, and the lawyer's tracks and identity are swallowed up in the personality of the former.

The lawyer's opportunities for good and for evil, are powerfully illustrated, in each and every step, in a litigation. His education, his training, his knowledge of the true objects, scope and influence of his profession, are all brought into play.

Is it not of paramount importance that individuals who are clothed with such extensive powers, should be fully instructed, in all of their duties and functions, before they are permitted to exercise them?

Picture the baleful influence upon the law and

society, of lawyers, clothed with so much power, badly educated, ignorant of the principles of law, and of the scope and objects of their profession, with minds not elevated, not ennobled, by liberal study or association! Picture the lawyers training themselves in a school of dishonesty, trickery, and chicanery, diverting and stopping the machinery of the law, prostituting the forms of justice for gain, selling their knowledge, ability, experience, and such talent as they may possess, to the client who pays most for the service, and resorting to every device of cunning and deceit, to gain their end! Do such lawyers exist? Do such practices prevail? Unfortunately, yes. In the first rank, in the middle rank, in the lowest rank of the profession, can be found many lawyers whose services are sought only to enable guilty men to escape punishment; only to open a door for others to avoid the consequence of the civil law, and of their contracts; only to defeat and evade the legislative will and public policy; only to show their clients how to cheat, defraud, vilify, and defame, without penalty or damage.

The formation of the Northern Securities Company under the laws of New Jersey, is a good illustration of one phase of the subject. A great moral responsibility rests upon the financial promoters of that Company. I do not undertake to measure or partition it. A consolidation of the railroads, embraced in that scheme, under the shallow pretense that the Northern Securities Company was a mere holding Company, was a clear attempt to evade the laws of the States through which the roads ran, and against the general public policy, and sentiment of the country.

The promoters sought to thwart the laws of those States, by going to the State of New Jersey, and organizing there. Not an individual really interested in the affair resided in New Jersey; not a penny's worth of property involved was located there; not a dollar of actual business was to be transacted there. The Anti-trust law of the United States stared them in the face in earnest protest against their acts; moreover, there were several clear decisions of the Supreme Court of the United States, which showed them that their work was illegal.[1] Yet they persevered, until their acts were overthrown by the Supreme Court of the United States. The promoters were, primarily, blamable in this matter, for they took their chances, hoping, through the ingenuity of their lawyers, or the slothfulness, neglect, or ignorance of public officials, to evade Statutes, and State and Federal

[1] U. S. v. Freight Assn., 166 U. S. 290; U. S. v. Joint Traffic Assn., 171 U. S. 505; Addyston Pipe & Steel Co. v. U. S., 175 U. S. 211; and others not necessary to quote.

policy. The decision of the four Judges in the lower court was unanimous against the Northern Securities Company, and although this judgment was only ratified in the Supreme Court of the United States by four votes against three—thus giving some pretense, or color, to the original scheme—yet this dissension would have been avoided, if the case had been thoroughly presented, on the part of the Government—I do not say it was inadequately presented by design—far from it—but, vital aspects of the question, not involved in a mere technical discussion, were overlooked. If the Northern Securities Company had been upheld as a legal corporation, it meant the placing of such untold power, in the hands of the promoters of the company, as would have enslaved the finances and commerce of the country. Examine its charter for confirmation of this result.

The statutes of New Jersey, themselves, stand as a shameful monument, to the cunning of the lawyers in an effort to resist National and State public policy. Almost every law of that State, in favor of corporations, has been craftily designed and built up, to cheat the general public policy of the country. The State coffers have been enriched by it; and each year new features are added to its corporation laws, to protect promoters, speculators, and majority shareholders. New Jersey, through her corporation law, has made herself an asylum, where rich and influential men, have sought refuge from the public policy of the law, and general sentiment of the community.

Finally, it is the attorney, as distinguished from the counselor, who can and does work the greater harm to the community. The business of the former is carried on in his office, away from the public gaze—his machinations are in the dark, and are insidious and secret. Shrouded in unlimited discretion, no one need know, but himself, how wantonly he is violating his duty, in the advice which he gives his client. It lies in his power always to say, "I was mistaken in the law or practice." The confused and contradictory condition, and accumulation of statute, and judge-made, law, is a perpetual asylum, to which the lawyers can resort, for justification, of all kinds of practices.

In the case of the counselor, he acts in the open—under the public gaze. His opportunities for accomplishing evil, are accordingly limited, to those cases where, by skill, art, experience, persuasion, or sophistry, he, unjustly, overcomes the judgment and minds of the courts or juries.

Public opinion is always on the alert, however, and by exposing and protesting, against unjust and illegal methods or results, in the court, it acts as a counterpoise to the meretricious influences of the dishonest advocate, and when the time comes, as a corrective. It is to be remembered, that all abuses inhering in any body of men, grow and strengthen, from the feeling of immunity from danger, with which they may be practiced. Insensible or scornful of extraneous opinion, they bury themselves within themselves, so to speak, and thus blindly invite a sometimes very rude form of resurrection.

One of the profoundest and most powerful reasons for divorcing the two branches of the profession arises from the above considerations. The work of the attorney must, where there are solicitors and barristers, pass through the hands of an independent counselor, who, necessarily, sits in judgment upon the facts and law before they are presented to the court. He acts as a breakwater between the attorney and the court. A litigant would be thus compelled to cross two barriers before he could reach the court. The attorney would no longer be allowed to prosecute, or defend, his own cases in court, and necessarily many dishonest, or illegal claims, would become abortive by the refusal of an independent counselor to present them.

The names "Attorney and Counselor" are still preserved in this country, although they represent practically one office.

F

Here, the lawyer is both an attorney and counselor.

As popularly understood, the attorney's practice comprehends all the business of the lawyer, transacted outside of the precincts of the court.

As counsel, he acts in a more limited, but, as it is generally understood, a higher capacity. First, as the word implies, in a purely advisory relation to his client; and, second, in becoming the mouthpiece of his client in court,—where he acts directly under the influence of the judges.

In both relations, therefore, free scope is given to his best endowments, his learning, experience, wisdom, genius, and eloquence.

He is also constantly called upon to exercise the best qualities of trained diplomacy, in the negotiations attending the settlement of difficult questions, in the best interest of parties, whose excited passions, have to be considered, at every step.

By virtue of his official character as attorney and counselor, the lawyer draws to himself a multitude of other employments, not strictly of a technical nature—that is, which do not grow out of misunderstandings, or contests, to be settled in court.

He is employed as agent, as attorney in fact,

trustee, executor, administrator, and in a thousand and one other fiduciary relations, which the ramifications and necessities of business create. A large share of this part of the lawyer's business, however, as I have shown,[1] has been gradually usurped by corporations, and, an extensive field of employment, removed from his control.

The lawyer appears everywhere, and in all stages of business transactions, and there is hardly an event of any magnitude in commercial affairs, in which his co-operation and counsel are not solicited.

His knowledge, judgment, experience, cleverness, and skill, are constantly drawn upon by his clients, who generally repose in their lawyers the utmost faith and confidence. He is in business, family, and other private and delicate matters, the trusted adviser and friend of his client, and is often consulted when the thoughts of the latter are in a chrysalis state, and he becomes an important factor in moulding his client's final judgment.

The confidence thus reposed is guarded, not only by the moral etiquette of the profession, but by positive statutory rules. It constitutes the most sacred part of the lawyer's functions. That it shall continue in its integrity is an im-

[1] Ante, p. 46.

portant interest of society, and it behooves society, for its own sake, that it should not assist in breaking it down, by vulgar and indiscriminate abuse of the character and functions of the lawyer as such.

CHAPTER VII.

THE LAWYER'S POLITICAL EMPLOYMENT AS A LEGIS-
LATOR, AND IN OTHER CAPACITIES. THE DUTIES
OF A LEGISLATOR.

EASILY, the most interesting relation, which a lawyer holds to the community, outside of his technical occupation, is that of a legislator.

From the commencement of the government, the lawyers have absolutely dominated in the Federal and State Legislatures. As I have said, they were the chief authors of the Constitution of the United States, and of all the State Constitutions. They are the natural and necessary interpreters of it; the guardians of it.

In the analysis, therefore, of the lawyer's relation to the community, it becomes of paramount importance to consider the duty and functions of a legislator. The forty-five State legislative mills (another has been since added to the list) are constantly grinding out Statutes,—useless and incoherent Statutes, most of them—and the Congress of the United States is engaged in the same occupation. Laws have accumulated, with such rapidity, that the jurisprudence of the United States is in a condition approaching inextricable confusion and doubt. The remark is applicable to constitutional, commercial, and criminal, as well as all of the other, branches of the law. The subject requires separate treatment. This state of affairs produces two principal results: first, it entails upon litigants and the Federal and State Governments, enormous expense amounting to many, many, millions each year; and, in the second place, it creates such uncertainty in the law as, practically, to make justice a thing of doubt and chance. To remedy these anomalous conditions, it is necessary that we should have legislators who understand their functions. I can only say, in this connection, that the responsibility for all of this unnecessary accumulation of Statutes rests somewhere. Primarily, it must be charged to the individuals who make the laws,—the legislators,— the lawyers.

What, then, are the duties of a legislator?

What are the qualifications which he should necessarily possess?

Primarily, he should know the relation which a citizen bears to the State—of which he is a member.

He must understand the origin and purpose

of society—of the principles which underlie political governments—Federal—State—Municipal.

Looking back into a period before society was organized, when a man was assumed to be an absolutely free creature—unrestricted and uncontrolled in his actions—we find that it was impossible for him to live in a savage state, and for his own protection, comfort, and happiness, he more or less consciously, but voluntarily, relinquished his natural condition and liberty, and sought refuge in organized association with his fellow men.

This, briefly, is the supposed origin of human government.

So deeply has this view been rooted, in the human mind and experience, that, practically, natural liberty has ceased to exist—in fact, it, perhaps, never did exist; and, in the effort of the mind, to conceive a condition of natural unrestrained liberty, one is remitted to an age of poetry and myths.

For, when a person is born into the world, he *eo instanti*, becomes a subject of some government, without any choice or consent of his own at all. He may afterwards expatriate himself, and transfer his allegiance to another State, but he can never enjoy natural or absolute liberty— he can never divest himself entirely of civic homage, for, wherever he is born, or wherever he may roam, he is always amenable to some government. In a word, every babe is born into the world with a political halter around its neck.

But, notwithstanding this fact, the legislator must go back to the supposed origin of the social compact, because this forms the proper and only true basis of legislative operations. Apart from the impossibility of tracing the origin of Society, writers all, substantially, agree that there is an implied contract between the sovereignty and the individual, by which the former grants protection, and the latter gives allegiance.

This original social compact is very important, and, withal, very simple. The citizen says, "I will give up my natural liberty—I will bind myself to become a part of the State—I will support the State in all emergencies."

The State says, in reply, "In return for the abdication of your natural rights and freedom, I will protect you and your family and your property, and I will only restrain so much of your natural liberty, as is necessary to protect you, and your fellow citizens."

Hence, we can appreciate that most admirable definition of civil or political liberty, by Lieber: "The natural liberty of mankind so far restrained by human laws as is necessary for the good of society." Or, as Burke says, in substance, his rights are his advantages.

"Only so far restrained by human law as is necessary for the good of society!" Consequently, the citizen is to enjoy all of his natural liberty, except so far as restraint is necessary, for his own, and his fellow men's, protection.

Here is the secret—the corner stone—of all legislation.

No laws are to be passed except those necessary for the subject's protection, or distinct, unequivocal (not speculative, not partial) benefit or advantage. The fundamental idea is, to leave the citizen with as much natural liberty, as is compatible with the interests and protection of the other members of society. In fine, to make as few laws as possible; for, in all normal and sound conditions of society, that country is best governed which is least governed. The Government exists for the people, not the people for the Government.

A multiplicity of laws does not produce good government, but, on the contrary, annuls and destroys its efficacy. It introduces confusion and uncertainty, and wherever these elements exist, individuals evade and escape from the operation of laws.

Hence a legislator must keep constantly before him the origin and purpose of the social compact. He must ask himself, "Is this proposed law necessary? Is it just? Is it for the true interests of the people, or the greater portion of them? By passing it, shall I take away, unnecessarily, any portion of the natural liberty of the subject?"

As Montesquieu says:[1]

> "Elles doivent etre relative au *physique* du pays; au climat glacé, brûlant, ou tempéré; à la qualité du terrain, à sa situation, à sa grandeur; au genre de vie des peuples, laboureurs, chasseurs ou pasteurs; elles doivent se rapporter au degré de liberté que la constitution peut souffrir, à la religion des habitants, à leurs inclinations, à leurs richesses, à leur nombre, à leur commerce, à leurs moeurs, à leurs manieres. Enfin, elles ont des rapports entre elles; elles en ont avec leur origine, avec l'object du législateur, avec l'ordre des choses sur lesquelles elles sont éstablies; c'est dans toutes ces vues qu'il faut les considérer."

To answer, or decide, these questions, is not an easy task—it always involves a knowledge of the existing institutions and laws, the mischief involved, and whether the new or proposed law constitutes an adequate remedy; a study of each great leading industry and interest, and its relation to the others and the whole.

What learning—what experience—what industry, a lawyer requires who would faithfully

[1] "De L'Esprit Des Lois," Vol. 1, p. 106, Livre I, Chap. III, ed. 1799. A. Basle, 1799.

fulfill the duties of a legislator! And contrasted with this standard, how deficient the modern legislator is! How few there are of legislators in the Federal, or State Legislatures, who understand and fulfill their real duties. How many laws, which now confuse and perplex the lawyers, and judges, would have been avoided; how many thousands of books and statutes which now encumber the shelves of the Law Libraries, would have never existed—if these fundamental, but simple, rules had been observed in the education and selection of legislators?

"Let any man look upon all that has been done in this department and trace it to its sources. He would acknowledge that legislation, good or bad, springs from the Bar." [1]

And if this dictum be thought too broad, yet with every abatement that can be made, popular demand, exigencies of society or situation, the field of the lawyer's action is still enormous. Nothing is more instructive and interesting in this connection than the seventh chapter of the second book of Rousseau's "Du Contrat Social"—"Du Legislateur"—in which he exclaims: "Mais s'il est vrai qu'un grand prince est un homme rare, que sera-ce d'un grand législateur."

Having satisfied himself of the necessity, the utility, the justness of the law, the legislator must

[1] "Sharswood's Legal Ethics," p. 25.

then prepare it.   Here he has need of the greatest skill, experience, and knowledge.

Why is it that the most profound lawyers shrink from drawing statutes? Because there is no task so delicate and difficult.   What is the old law?   What is the evil?   What is the necessity?   What is the remedy proposed?   From the infinite catalogue of language, what words shall be selected to express accurately and clearly the thought, the principle, the facts, to be covered by the legislation?   Simplicity, precision, brevity, perfect clearness, must here be observed.

Another important feature of an American legislator is, that he must compare all proposed laws, with the Federal and State Constitutions.

This involves an accurate knowledge of these instruments.

To sum up: if a new law be proposed, the legislator must determine its necessity, its justness, in the light of the social compact above described, and of all the other considerations bearing upon the subject.[1]   If an amendment to an existing law be proposed, he must know the

[1] "La Loi, en général, est la raison humaine, en tant qu'elle gouverne tous les peuple de la terre; et les lois politique et civiles de chaque nation ne doivent être que les cas particuliers où s'applique cette raison humaine.

"Elles doivent être tellement propres au peuple pour lequel elles sont faitres, que c'est un très grand hasard si celles d'une nation peuvent convenir à une autre." Montesquieu, "De L'Esprit Des Lois," Livre I, Chap. III, pp. 135, ed. 1826.

old law, the mischief, and the remedy, and he must, finally, be able to put the proposed legislation into clear, unmistakable, and unequivocal language.

The failure to observe these rules, is the cause of all the unwise, voluminous, unnecessary, and unconstitutional legislation, which now fills our statute books and piles up our law books mountain high. I cite, below, a large number of cases which show how constantly the courts have been occupied, in the State of New York, alone, since 1862, in the work of declaring Statutes unconstitutional.[1]

[1] **1.** L. 1862, CHAP. 459.—Unconstitutional so far as it authorizes the seizure and sale, without judicial process, of animals found trespassing within a private inclosure.

Rockwell *v.* Nearing, 35 N. Y. 302.

2. L. 1862, CHAP. 482.—The act of 1862 providing for the collection of demands against vessels, so far as it gives a lien for supplies furnished to, or repairs made upon a vessel engaged in foreign commerce, is unconstitutional, and a bond given pursuant to the act to release a vessel detained by virtue of an attachment issued thereunder, is void.

Poole *v.* Kermit, 59 N. Y. 554.

3. L. 1863, SEC. 9, CHAP. 361.—"An act to authorize the construction of a railway and tracks in the towns of West Farms and Morrisania." Act unconstitutional in part.

Bohmer *v.* Haffen, 161 N. Y. 390.

4. L. 1866, CHAP. 217.—Section 1, of chapter 217 of laws of 1866, extending the term of the incumbents of the office of justice and clerk of the District Court of the eighth judicial district in the city of New York, is in conflict with section 18, of article 6, of the Constitution of 1846, and is void.

The People ex rel. *v.* Bull, 48 N. Y. 57.

When one adds to this record, the aggregate adjudications, of the Courts of all the States of the Union, and in the Federal Courts, to a like effect, the list becomes appalling.   Opening up further

5. L. 1866.—The provision of said act (Sec. 4) providing that on appeal from the award of commissioners, the court may increase or diminish the compensation, is violative of the constitutional provision (Art. 1, Sec. 7) declaring that the compensation for property taken for public use shall be ascertained by a jury or by commissioners.

In re Vil. Middletown, 82 N. Y. 196.

6. L. 1868.—Provided that the supervisors of the counties of Erie and Chautauqua should assess upon their respective counties a moiety of such further sum, not exceeding $10,000, as the said commissioners should certify to be necessary for the completion of the bridge, is unconstitutional and void.

People ex rel. Chas. H. Lee, etc., v. The Board of Supervisors of the County of Chautauqua, 43 N. Y. 10.

7. L. 1868.—An act of the legislature appropriating moneys from the capital of the common school fund, to the establishment of an astronomical observatory, is in violation of the Constitution (article 9), and void.

People v. Allen, 42 N. Y. 404.

8. L. 1869, CHAP. 84, SEC. 2.—A statute attempting to validate a void subscription to capital stock of railroad unconstitutional.

N. Y. & O. M. R. R. Co. v. Van Horn, 57 N. Y. 473.

9. L. 1869, CHAP. 217, SEC. 4.—Amended by CHAP. 619, LAWS of 1870.   A law imposing an assessment for a local improvement without notice to, and a hearing, or an opportunity to be heard, on the part of the owner of the property to be assessed, has the effect to deprive him of his property without due process of law and is unconstitutional.

Stuart v. Palmer, 74 N. Y. 183.

10. L. 1870, CHAP. 77, TIT. 7, SEC. 1.—The provision of the act of 1870 in relation to the city of Albany prescribing that, for the pur-

investigation, into the history of the enactment and repeal of unnecessary statutes, one is tempted to exclaim: "How much longer can this nation bear the staggering burden of such ignorant legis-

pose of ascertaining the compensation to be paid by said city to the owners of lands taken for streets, etc., the common council shall nominate twelve freeholders whose names, on separate ballots, are to be placed in a box, from whence are to be drawn three, who shall be appointed commissioners, etc., is unconstitutional, and proceedings taken thereunder void.

Menges v. City of Albany, 56 N. Y. 374.

11. L. 1870, CHAP. 291.—TITLE 7, p. 694 (Village Act), as amended by L. 1878, Chap. 59, p. 66 (right of appeal from award of jury of damages for street opening on giving bond for costs) invalid—as taking without process.

People v. Board, 151 N. Y. 75.

12. L. 1870, CHAP. 291.—TITLE 7, p. 694, as amended by L. 1893, Chap. 694, prescribing qualifications for a jury to assess damages for street opening invalid—as such a jury is not that required by Constitution.

People v. Board, 151 N. Y. 75.

13. L. 1870, CHAP. 365, SEC. 2, as amended by L. 1894, CHAP. 622.—Crime for city contractor to employ alien, void as infringing personal rights and due process of law.

People v. Warren, 34 N. Y. S. 942.

14. L. 1871, CHAP. 809.—Legislature has no power to impose debt on town without consent.

See Horton v. Town of Thompson, 71 N. Y. 513.

15. L. 1871, CHAP. 810.—Amendment to L. 1869, CHAP. 714. The provision of said amendment confirming the acts of the common council theretofore done in reference to the construction of sewers did not validate the assessment, as the section itself, so far as it relates to the confirmation of assessments, was unconstitutional and void.

City of Watertown v. Jason Fairbanks, 65 N. Y. 588.

lation and judicial conflict!" Justinian's task in reforming the Roman Law, one of the greatest undertakings of ancient history, was a pastime, compared to the herculean labor which is devolved upon the lawyers of the twentieth century.

16. L. 1873, CHAP. 452.—The provision of the act of 1873 authorizing the taking of lands for the purpose of such an association, by proceeding in invitum, is unconstitutional and void.

In re D. C. Assn., 66 N. Y. 569.

17. L. 1874, CHAP. 545, SEC. 4.—That provision of the act relating to the Marine Court of the city of New York authorizing any court of record to transfer an action pending therein to the Marine Court, and thereupon giving the latter exclusive jurisdiction thereof, is unconstitutional, and an order made by the Superior Court for the purpose of making such a transfer was void.

Alexander v. Bennett, 60 N. Y. 204.

18. L. 1876, CODE CIV. PROC., SEC. 758.—Providing that estate of a joint contractor shall not be discharged upon his death, does not affect contracts made prior to its passage.

Randall v. Sackett, 77 N. Y. 480.

19. L. 1879, CODE CIV. PROC., SEC. 856.—Committal for contempt for refusal to answer controller's questions, void, as depriving of liberty without process.

In re Grout, 93 N. Y. S. 711.

20. L. 1880.—The provision of the act of 1880 (SEC. 4, CHAP. 59, LAWS of 1880) for the relief of the Manhattan Savings Institution, which by its terms discharges the city of Yonkers, upon delivery by it to said institution of duplicate bonds, from liability upon certain negotiable bonds issued by it "to all persons purchasing the same after due publication of the notice specified in the first section of this act" is unconstitutional, as the effect thereof is to destroy the negotiable quality of the bonds, and so it impairs the obligation of contracts.

People ex rel. v. Otis, 90 N. Y. 48.

The legislator should, therefore, be a man who understands the origin and nature of society— familiar with past and existing laws and history —with such practical and discriminating judg-

21. L. 1880, CHAP. 582.—As applicable to such a road, therefore, the provision of the act of 1880 in reference to underground street railways, declaring that the determination of commissioners, confirmed by the court, " may be taken in lieu of the consent of said authorities," is unconstitutional and invalid.

In re N. Y. Dist. R. R. Co., 107 N. Y. 42.

22. L. 1881, CHAP. 532.—Purporting to amend the provision of the Code of Civil Procedure (Sec. 1041) in regard to the selection and drawing of jurors in the city and county of Albany. Assuming the said act not to have been reported by the commissioners appointed by law to revise the statutes, and so not within the exception (Art. 3, Sec. 25) exempting from the operation of said provisions bills so reported, the said act is, as to grand jurors, unconstitutional and void.

People v. Petrea, 92 N. Y. 128.

23. L. 1881, CHAP. 637.—The provision of the act of 1881 purporting to authorize the E. B. W. & M. Co. to acquire title to lands by proceedings in invitum, was unconstitutional and void.

In re Eureka Basin, etc., 96 N. Y. 42.

24. CODE CIV. PROC. (SEC. 1440), relating to title to real property sold on execution, as amended in 1881 (Chap. 681, Laws of 1881). The legislature has no power to deny, for any cause, to a party who has been illegally deprived of his property, access to the constitutional courts of the State for relief.

Gilman v. Tucker, 128 N. Y. 190.

25. L. 1882, CHAP. 92.—Act prohibiting Turnpike Co. from charging toll for bicycles held unconstitutional as taking of property without due process of law.

Rochester & C. Turnpike Road Co. v. Joel, 58 N. Y. S. 346.

26. L. 1882, CHAP. 410, SEC. 677.—The provision of the New York Consolidation Act which declares that no compensation shall be al-

G

ment as enables him to comprehend the wants and necessities of his fellow men. In this respect, it is, in some aspects, a higher term than even statesman. Suppose the Bar would seriously

lowed to the owner of land taken for a street for any building erected or placed thereon after the filing of a map of the street as prescribed by the Act (Sec. 672), by its terms imposes a restriction upon the use of the land which amounts to an incumbrance, and so is unconstitutional.

Foster v. Scott, 136 N. Y. 577.

27. L. 1884, CHAP. 60.—A statute cutting down the right to commence an action upon a cause of action then existing, from a period without limitation to a few months after the passage of the act, does not give such reasonable time, and so is unconstitutional.

Parmenter v. The State of N. Y., 135 N. Y. 154.

28. L. 1884, CHAP. 202, SEC. 4.—A legislative enactment which absolutely prohibits an important branch of industry, not injurious to the community, and not fraudulently conducted, solely for the reason that it competes with another, and may reduce the price of an article of food, is unconstitutional.

People v. Marx, 99 N. Y. 377.

29. L. 1884, CHAP. 272.—The act entitled " An act to improve the public health, by prohibiting the manufacture of cigars and preparation of tobacco in any form in tenement houses, in certain cases," etc., is unconstitutional.

In re Jacobs, 98 N. Y. 98.

30. L. 1885.—CODE CIV. PROC., SEC. 90, so far as it prohibits a Court of Common Pleas from appointing its clerk as a referee is unconstitutional.

Popfinger v. Yutte, 102 N. Y. 38.

31. L. 1885, CHAP. 183.—In order to sustain an indictment under the provision of the act of 1885 (Sec. 7, Chap. 183, Laws of 1885, amended by chap. 458, Laws of 1885), prohibiting the manufacture or sale of any article " not produced from unadulterated milk, or cream

throw its whole influence to prevent the election of individuals to the Legislature, who did not substantially fulfill these requirements. Would not the community at once feel the benefit of such a

from the same," which is " in imitation or semblance of or designed to take the place of butter," it must be made to appear that the article manufactured was, by the use of ingredients, not necessary or essential to the article itself, made in imitation or semblance of butter; the manufacture of an article simply "designed to take the place of butter" is not an offense, as so much of the provision is unconstitutional.

People *v.* Arensburg, 103 N. Y. 388.

32. L. 1886, CHAP. 271 and CHAP. 310.—The acts of 1886 providing, in case of such a dissolution for the taking away from the company of its street franchises, and for the winding up of its affairs by suit brought by the attorney general, and the appointment of a receiver therein, are unconstitutional and void.

People *v.* O'Brien, 111 N. Y. 1.

33. SECTION 1421, CODE OF CIVIL PROCEDURE, amended in 1887. Substitution of indemnitor in action against sheriff. Unconstitutionality of Mandatory Provision.

Levy *v.* Dunn, 160 N. Y. 504.

34. L. 1887, CHAP. 627.—The provision of the act of 1887 confirming sales of land for the nonpayment of taxes theretofore made under the act of 1874, authorizing sales of lands for unpaid taxes in the county of Westchester (Chap. 610, Laws of 1874), so far as it seeks to validate a sale, void because made under a void assessment, is unconstitutional.

Cromwell *v.* MacLean, 123 N. Y. 474.

35. L. 1887, CHAP. 688.—Penal Code Sec. 171a, compelling employee not to join labor organizations, a misdemeanor, void, as deprivation of equal protection of laws.

People *v.* Marcus, 97 N. Y. S. 322, 185 N. Y. 257.

36. L. 1887, CHAP. 691.—The provision of the Penal Code (Sec. 335a, added by Chap. 691, Laws of 1887) prohibiting the sale or disposal of

movement? But where would they find them? How are they to be known? When found and known, how are they to be made available in a system like ours? These are the real questions. With-

any article of food, or any offer or attempt to do so upon any representation or inducement that anything else will be delivered as a gift, prize, premium or reward to the purchaser, is unconstitutional and void.

People *v.* Gillson, 109 N. Y. 389.

37. The Provision of the Code of Civil Procedure (Sec. 1582, as amended by Chap. 39, Laws of 1889) authorizing the Special Term, in an action for partition, in which a portion of the proceeds of a sale has been paid into court or deposited with the county treasurer for unknown heirs and twenty-five years have elapsed without any claim being made therefor by any person entitled thereto, "to decree that such unclaimed portion of such proceeds was vested at the time of such payment in the known heirs of the common ancestor of such unknown heirs and their heirs and assigns" is unconstitutional.

People ex rel *v.* Ryder, 124 N. Y. 500.

38. L. 1889, Chap. 382, Constitution, Art. 3, Sec. 29.—Prohibiting work by convict for sale is invalid as to contracts made prior to Constitution.

Bronk *v.* Barckley, 43 N. Y. S. 400.

39. L. 1890, Chap. 294, Sec. 59.—Amended by L. 1893, Chap. 190. Charter of Schenectady, requiring assessment for street paving to be apportioned according to foot frontage, is void as taking without process.

Conde *v.* City, 164 N. Y. 258.

40. L. 1890, Chap. 400 (Insurance Law 1892, Sec. 56).—Providing that no one but Attorney General shall proceed against insurance company, void, as to policy holder who became such power to act.

Greel *v.* Equitable, 57 N. Y. S. 871.

out an intentional impeachment of the form of democratic government, it is nevertheless true, that prototypes of the best class of legislators, do not always appear, in the recognized legislative assemblies.

41. L. 1892, CHAP. 214.—Conferring upon women the right to vote for school commissioners is unconstitutional.

In re Gage, 141 N. Y. 112.

42. L. 1892, CHAP. 467, SEC. 2.—As to committal of female inebriates without judicial trial, void, as taking without due process.

People v. St. Saviours San., 56 N. Y. S. 8, 431.

43. L. 1892, CHAP. 488, SECS. 110, 112.—Misdemeanor to possess fish during certain seasons and inflicting penalty, void as to imported fish, as taking without process.

People v. Buffalo, 62 N. Y. S. 543, 1143.

44. L. 1892, CHAP. 664.—Unconstitutionality of act for payments to drafted men by taxation.

Bush v. Board of Supervisors, 159 N. Y. 212.

45. L. 1892, CHAP. 687, SEC. 15.—Prohibiting suits by foreign corporations without a certificate, void, as denying equal protection of laws.

Hargreaves v. Harden, 56 N. Y. S. 937.

46. L. 1892, CHAP. 690.—A statute making void a contract entered into by a citizen of one State with a corporation of another, made and to be performed in the latter, insuring property within the former State, is void under Const. U. S., Amend. 14.

West. Mass. Mut. Fire Ins. Co. v. Hilton, 58 N. Y. S. 996.

47. L. 1893, CHAP. 338.—AGRICULTURAL LAW, SEC. 50, defining adulterated vinegar, and that cider vinegar made by State farms shall not be deemed such, void as discriminating.

People v. Windholz, 86 N. Y. S. 1015.

48. L. 1893, CHAP. 376.—Authorizing construction of a cremator for destruction of garbage, etc., unconstitutional as not providing

There are epochs in all governments, when its official servants, fail to respond, to ideal requirements. But a democracy offers practical, and the readiest, methods of correcting such evils.

compensation to adjoining owners affected by offensive stenches from the cremator.

Kobbe *v.* Village, 45 N. Y. S. 777.

49. CONST. 1894, ART. 1, SEC. 7.—Authorized occupants of agricultural lands to construct ditches on lands of others on compensating them, violates Const. U. S., Art. 14, taking without process.

In re Tuthill, 163 N. Y. 133.

50. L. 1894, CHAP. 284.—Permitting water corporations to arbitrarily assess for water rates, void, as impairing obligation of contracts.

Warsaw *v.* Village, 161 N. Y. 176.

51. L. 1851, CHAP. 307, Amended by L. 1894, CHAP. 712.—Declaring Moose River a public highway for floating logs, void, as failing to provide compensation to owners for land taken in improving river.

De Camp *v.* Thompson, 44 N. Y. 1014.

52. L. 1895, CHAP. 162.—Trial court will not declare act unconstitutional unless there can be no reasonable doubt on the subject.

City of Ithaca *v.* Babcock, 72 N. Y. S. 519.

53. L. 1895, CHAP. 342.—Authorizing a pardoned convict to sue for damages, although judgment against him unreversed, invalid, as being an exercise of judicial functions.

Roberts *v.* State, 51 N. Y. S. 691.

54. L. 1895, CHAP. 417.—Free transportation in street railroads for policemen, void, as beyond police power.

Wilson *v.* Traction Co., 76 N. Y. S. 203.

55. L. 1895, CHAP. 559, SEC. 47.—Authorizing a cemetery association to make rules and to collect penalties for non-observance, unlaw-

If the lawyers are to continue as our principal legislators, they must be educated up to the standards of their real functions, powers, and duties; the legitimate effect of which will be to ful, as legislature without power to give such authority to a non-governmental agency.

Johnstown v. Parker, 59 N. Y. S. 821, 60 N. Y. S. 1015.

56. L. 1895, CHAP. 633.—No action against warehouseman unless he has claim other than for charges, void, as taking without process.

Follet v. Albany, 70 N. Y. S. 474; Milligan v. Co., 68 N. Y. S. 744.

57. L. 1895, CHAP. 792.—Protection of holders of municipal negotiable bonds by giving right of appeal to Court of Appeals although amount in controversy less than $500, void as to retroactive operation.

Germania S. Bank v. Village, 159 N. Y. 362.

58. L. 1895, CHAP. 1027, SEC. 1.—Making railroad liable to a penalty for refusing to sell 1,000-mile ticket at reduced rate, void, as outside police power, discriminating, and taking without process.

Beardsley v. N. Y., 162 N. Y. 230.

59. L. 1896, CHAP. 22, SECS. 19 and 20.—Unconstitutionality of Abolition of Justices' criminal jurisdiction—Town of Fort Edward.

People ex rel. Barby v. Howland, 155 N. Y. 270.

60. L. 1893, CHAP. 601, as amended by L. 1896, CHAP. 272.—Prohibiting marriage of uncle and niece, not retroactive.

Weisberg v. Weisberg, 98 N. Y. S. 260.

61. L. 1896, CHAP. 378, SECS. 707, 711.—Giving workhouse superintendent power to determine imprisonment of one committed for intoxication, invalid as without due process.

In re Kenny, 49 N. Y. S. 1037; People v. Cheamer, 53 N. Y. S. 1111.

62. L. 1896, CHAP. 383.—Protection of Oysters—Forfeiture of disturbing vessel. Unconstitutional.

Colon v. Lish, 153 N. Y. 188.

give us a new and different class of officials. In the present system of education of the lawyer, these essentials are not in his curriculum.

If the moral sense of the community, which

63. L. 1896, CHAP. 427.—Unconstitutional restriction upon appointment to office. Invalidation of entire act by inseparable constitutional provision.

Rathbone v. Wirth, 150 N. Y. 459.

64. L. 1896.—License fees are public moneys. Appropriation to private corporation—Chapter 446, unconstitutional.

Fox v. Mohawk & H. R. Humane Society, 165 N. Y. 517.

65. L. 1896, CHAP. 529, SEC. 82.—Forty-eight hours' notice to village clerk of a village of intention to sue village for personal injuries, void, as unreasonable and taking without process.

Green v. Village, 64 N. Y. S. 547.

66. L. 1896, CHAP. 545.—Insanity Law permitting perpetual confinement of one as insane without notice or hearing at which he is present, void, as depriving of liberty without process.

People v. Wendel, 68 N. Y. S. 948.

67. L. 1893, CHAP. 452, and L. 1896, CHAP. 547, SEC. 83.—Empowering beneficiary of a trust to terminate trust without consent of trustee, void, as taking without process.

Oviatt v. Hopkins, 46 N. Y. S. 959.

68. L. 1896, CHAP. 727.—Authorizing condemnation for a park, void as taking without process, there being no provision for notice.

In re City, 70 N. Y. S. 227.

69. L. 1896, CHAP. 772.—Kings County—District Attorney, providing that district attorneys of Kings County shall be elected every four years.

People ex rel. Eldred v. Palmer, 154 N. Y. 133.

70. L. 1896, CHAP. 803.—Prohibiting a firm to do business in New York City as master plumbers unless its members shall have been registered after examination by the examining board of plumbis another name for public opinion, should be maintained to the highest possible degree, an educated Bar, and a free, pure and intelligent, Press, are the factors which can do much to accomplish all these results.

ers, void, as prohibiting formation of a partnership to carry on a lawful business.

Schnaier v. Navarre, 182 N. Y. 83.

71. L. 1896, CHAP. 931.—Unconstitutionality of convict-made goods, label act—Interstate Commerce.

People v. Hawkins, 157 N. Y. 1.

72. L. 1897, CHAP. 284.—Transfer Tax act does not apply to a property acquired prior to its passage.

In re Lansing's Est., 182 N. Y. 238.

73. L. 1897, CHAP. 415, ART. 8, SEC. 110.—Limiting employment in bakeries to 10 hours a day and 60 hours a week, void, as outside police power.

Loehner v. People, 76 N. Y. S. 396.

74. L. 1897, CHAP. 415, SECS. 180, 184.—Requiring horseshoers to be examined and to obtain a certificate, etc., void, as interference without due process.

People v. Beattie, 89 N. Y. S. 193.

75. L. 1897, CHAP. 415, PENAL CODE, SEC. 384, SUBD. 1.—Hours of labor under contracts with State or municipalities, void, as discriminating.

People v. Orange, 175 N. Y. 84.

76. L. 1893, CHAP. 452; L. 1896, CHAPS. 547, 553; and L. 1897, CHAP. 417, SEC. 3.—Permitting life beneficiary of trust of personalty who becomes entitled to remainder, to end the trust, not retroactive as to trusts created before their enactment.

Newcomb v. Newcomb, 68 N. Y. S. 430.

77. L. 1897, CHAP. 506.—Unconstitutionality of Act limiting sale of Passage Tickets.

People ex rel. Tyroler v. Warden, etc., 157 N. Y. 116.

Turning from legislative to other fields, we find that the lawyers occupy almost the entire horizon, of the official world.

The eye cannot be opened upon any department

78. L. 1898.—An amendatory act passed in 1898 to the Turnpike Act (L. 1847, Chap. 210), by which a company's earnings are reduced 25%, void, as impairing obligation of a contract.

Rochester v. Joel, 58 N. Y. S. 346.

79. L. 1899, TAX, CHAP. 76, LAWS OF 1899.—Imposing transfer tax upon remainders or reversions vesting prior to June 30, 1885, unconstitutional.

Matter of Pell, 171 N. Y. 48.

80. L. 1897, CHAP. 415; L. 1899, CHAPS. 192, 567.—That laborers on public works be paid prevailing rate of wages, etc., void, as taking away liberty of free contract.

People v. Coler, 166 N. Y. 1.

81. L. 1899.—Statute requiring appointment of person highest on list, unconstitutional.—Chap. 370, 13.

People ex rel. Balcom v. Mosher, 162 N. Y. 32.

82. L. 1899, CHAP. 502.—CODE, SEC. 920, providing for committal of witness before commissioner of foreign court, invalid, as against due process.

People v. Leubischer, 51 N. Y. S. 735, 54 N. Y. S. 869.

83. L. 1899, CHAP. 567.—Repealing all prior statutes as to securing prevailing rate of wages to municipal employees—void as to claim of workman employed prior to repealing statute.

McCann v. City, 52 App. 358.

84. L. 1899, CHAP. 700.—Providing that municipal corporations shall pay the expenses of a person who has been indicted within its boundaries for a criminal offense in connection with his official duties, is unconstitutional.

In re Straus (Sup.), 61 N. Y. S. 37; In re Fallon, 59 N. Y. S. 849.

of the Federal, State, or Municipal governments, without encountering them.

They, naturally, engross all of the judicial offices, and they swarm everywhere, in the legislative and executive branches of the government.

85. L. 1900, AMENDING CHARTER N. Y. SEC. 1212.—Prohibiting boiling of garbage, void, as taking without process.

New York v. Department, 70 N. Y. S. 510.

86. L. 1900, CHAP. 534.—Agricultural Law, Sec. 27, as amended by L. 1900, prohibiting sale of butter or cheese containing a preservative, etc., void, as not proper exercise of police power.

People v. Biesecker, 68 N. Y. 1067.

87. L. 1900, CHAP. 614.—Providing that a county should pay a bank its defaulting treasurer's overdraft, although a judgment had been given in favor of county in action by bank, void, as depriving county of a vested right.

Greene v. Niagara, 166 N. Y. 485.

88. L. 1900.—Judgment for alimony constitutes property of wife of which she cannot be deprived without due process of law— Chap. 742—in so far as it affects prior judgments for, unconstitutional.

Livingston v. Livingston, 173 N. Y. 377, 77 N. Y. Sup. 476; Goodsell v. Goodsell, 81 N. Y. S. 806.

89. L. 1897, CHAP. 418, as amended by L. 1900, CHAP. 762.—Providing for sale by auction by vendor, and, in default, recovery of moneys paid by vendee, void as to sales prior to its passage.

Hæfelein v. Jacob, 94 N. Y. S. 466.

90. L. 1901, CHAP. 128.—Amending Penal Code SEC. 640d, providing that in cities of the first and second class persons offering real property for sale without written authority from vendor or vendee, guilty of misdemeanor, void, as taking without process.

Cody v. Dempsey, 83 N. Y. S. 899; Grossman v. Caminez, 79 App. Div. 15; Contra, Whiteley v. Terry, 78 N. Y. S. 911.

Individuals imbibe from the lawyer notions of the principles of government; they hear from him the reasons for new, and the motives for alterations of old, laws; they readily accept his

91. L. 1897, CHAP. 378, amended by L. 1901, CHAP. 469, SEC. 1560.—Forbidding city pensioners to hold city employment, void, as against abridgment of citizens' privileges (Const. 1894, Art. 1, sec. 1).

People *v.* Woodbury, 77 N. Y. S. 241.

92. L. 1899, CHAP. 451, as amended by L. 1901, CHAP. 503.—Relief of banks as to lost certificates of deposit, void so far as retroactive.

In re Cook, 83 N. Y. S. 100.

93. L. 1901, CHAP. 639.—Preventing any than common carriers from engaging in ticket brokerage business, void, as taking without process.

People *v.* Caldwell, 168 N. Y. 671.

94. L. 1896, CHAP. 112, as amended by L. 1901, CHAP. 640.—For canceling of license certificate unless holder files an answer denying violation, void, as taking without due process.

In re Cullman, 81 N. Y. S. 567.

95. Act Jan. 22, 1902.—Providing that Act April 25, 1901, giving salary to Alderman, but for no part of 1901, void, as impairing a vested right.

Young *v.* City, 76 N. Y. S. 224.

96. L. 1902, p. 1367.—Section of charter of city of Middletown providing that written notice of dangerous condition of sidewalk must be given to city before recovery can be had for personal injuries, void, as taking away right of action altogether.

MacMullen *v.* City, 92 N. Y. S. 410, 98 N. Y. S. 145.

97. L. 1902, CHAP. 94, CODE CIV. PROC., SEC. 618.—Citizen of N. Y. compelled to attend, on subpœna, criminal procedure in Pennsylvania, void, as depriving of liberty without process.

In re Commonwealth, 90 N. Y. S. 808.

technical explanations of the causes and effects of legislation, when not of a purely partisan character.[1]

In times of excitement, when public resent-

98. L. 1902, CHAP. 194, SEC. 141.—Prohibiting possession in close season of trout taken outside the State, void, as infringing liberty and property rights, and as beyond police power.

People *v.* Booth Co., 86 N. Y. S. 272.

99. L. 1897, CHAP. 414, SEC. 230, amended by L. 1902, CHAP. 591. —Providing that buildings within 500 feet of hydrant may be assessed although water not used, void, as taking without process.

Village of Canaseraga *v.* Green, 88 N. Y. S. 539.

100. L. 1902, CHAP. 608.—Warehouseman may refuse to deliver goods to holder of receipt when another claims them, and that he shall not be made defendant in action unless he claims interest, void, as taking without process.

97 N. Y. S. 227.

101. L. 1903, CHAP. 137.—Commutation for good behavior only allowed to convict committed on definite sentence, void, as to offenses committed prior to its passage.

People *v.* Johnson, 90 N. Y. S. 134.

102. L. 1903, CHAP. 272.—Amending Penal Code, 640, Subd. 16, prohibiting use of United States and State Flags for advertisement, unconstitutional in part.

People ex rel. McPike *v.* Van De Carr, 178 N. Y. 425.

103. L. 1903, CHAP. 461, CODE CIV. PROC., SEC. 1391.—As amended by L. 1903, special execution against income or profits of judgment debtor, void, as to trusts created before its passage.

Sloane *v.* Tiffany, 93 N. Y. S. 149; King *v.* Irving, 92 N. Y. S. 1094.

---

[1] " The scattering of men who are taught reverence for existing institutions among the mass of the people is of incalculable benefit in preserving order, property, and propagating a respect for obedience to the law on the part of the other members of the community." De Tocqueville, Vol. I, p. 348.

ment or passion is aroused, the lawyer's influence ought to be great. He becomes a breakwater between the passions of excited citizens, and the forms and rules of the law.

His trained habits of thought, his respect for the law, his devotion to existing rules and forms, all combine to make him a power of great impor-

104. L. 1904.—Privilege of witness provided for by Section 342 of the Penal Code not coextensive with that afforded by constitutional provision.

People ex rel. Lewisohn v. O'Brien, 176 N. Y. 253.

105. L. 1904, CHAP. 173, CODE CIV. PROC., SEC. 793.—As amended by L. 1904, Chap. 173, requiring courts in certain districts to arbitrarily regulate preference of causes, void, as depriving judiciary of right to regulate the hearing by the circumstances of each case.

Riglander v. Star Co., 90 N. Y. S. 772 ; aff'd, 181 N. Y. 531.

106. L. 1904, CHAP. 657.—Regulating trading stamps, void, as outside police power.

People v. Zimmerman, 92 N. Y. S. 497.

107. About 1904.—Municipal ordinance allowing projections beyond building line, void, as taking without process.

McMillan v. Klaw, 95 N. Y. S. 365.

108.—Proposed amendment of charter of a corporation, L. 1853, Chap. 463, organizing the Equitable Life Assurance Co., changing method of electing directorate, void, as taking without process.

Lord v. Equitable, 94 N. Y. S. 65. (May 26, 1905.)

109. L. 1905, CHAP. 697.—Authorizing special deputy commissioner to revoke liquor tax license issued prior to passage, void, as taking without process.

People v. Flynn, 96 N. Y. S. 655.

I pause here. There are some thirty-five additional acts declared unconstitutional in the State of New York. Space will not permit me to print them; besides, the list is already nauseatingly long.

tance, in these dangerous emergencies. As a voluntary instructor, his advice and judgment are received without suspicion or reserve. As the maxim still prevails that every man is presumed to know the law, the occupation of a lawyer, in his social sphere, as a free and voluntary promulgator of it, becomes one of great importance.

The influence, of this body of calm, intelligent, and trained oracles of the law, mingling without reserve among all classes, is always in proportion to the respect with which they are held by the community. Judge Sharswood [1] says:

> "It is its office (the Bar) to diffuse sound principles among the people, that they may intelligently exercise the controlling power placed in their hands, in the choice of their representatives in the legislature, and of judgment in deciding, as they are often called upon to do, upon the most important changes in the Constitution, and above all, in the formation of that public opinion which may be said in these times almost without a figure, to be ultimate sovereign."

The characteristics of the lawyers are identical everywhere. Without premeditated or concerted action, they instinctively act together in defense of fundamental principles of liberty, justice, and religion. They have the same training; they

[1] Legal Ethics, p. 54.

are taught to observe form and order; to determine questions by certain fixed principles, based upon the fundamental maxims of social and political right; to respect and preserve precedents and existing institutions; to guard sacredly the rights of persons and property; and the general similarity of their habits of thought instinctively converts them into champions of fixed principles, as opposed to temporary make-shifts and frothy declamation. Yet they rarely act as an organized body—never, in a truly political sense.

De Tocqueville asserts [1] that, in all "free" governments, of whatsoever form they may be, the members of the legal profession will be found at the head of all political parties. This is undoubtedly true, in the broadest sense, so far as the government of the United States is concerned, of which he was writing. But in England, which is certainly "free," no such exclusive privilege exists. I cannot recall an instance, where a pure lawyer has been a great leader in the House of Commons, or even very great in Parliamentary debate. Mansfield was noted in his time. Perhaps Brougham comes nearest to it, but then, he was not a "pure" lawyer. Some have been great there when charged with a special mission, like Sir Samuel Romilly, but that is different. The

[1] "Democracy in America," p. 350.

truth seems to be that the influence of the lawyers in England, when not strictly official, has been of the subtle kind—advocates and champions of justice, which, when best administered, means the highest state of civilization.

In the United States, on the other hand, the instincts, education, and training of the lawyers fit and adapt them for political life, and from the beginning of the government they have almost exclusively occupied the leadership of political parties.

A comparison between the English and American Statesmen and orators, in the aspect in which I am here considering them, furnishes a most striking picture of the difference between the two governments.

The interpretation of a written Constitution, from which most of our political history takes its origin, *ex necessitate rei*, brings into public life a large body of lawyers—professional, technical, constructionists—to the substantial exclusion of the lay element of the community. The Constitution of the United States becomes the guide for most of our internal politics, and American politicians must study it, as the *sine qua non*, to political education and advancement. Except in rare cases, it seems that their political inspirations, and ideas, are limited and circumscribed, by that instrument. Even the tariff

H

legislation has been challenged, as contrary to the Constitution. In the United States, therefore, most of the greatest political acts, and efforts of eloquence, have been inaugurated and inspired by pure and technical constitutional lawyers; whereas in England, as early as 1628, when Sir John Eliot delivered his speech in the House of Commons, on the petition of rights, down to the present time, the great speeches have been almost universally made by trained statesmen, and political students, and the orations of Walpole, Chatham, Chesterfield, Burke, Fox, Pitt, Sheridan, Canning, and Gladstone and others are carefully studied, as models of wisdom and British eloquence.

In both countries, however, the sphere of the lawyer's influence has been unlimited, and in public and private life he has been a factor of the greatest importance, in the administration of all branches of the governments.

CHAPTER VIII.

THE OBLIGATIONS OF A LAWYER.

I HAVE heretofore, briefly, sketched the system under which the lawyer is educated; the limitations upon his right to practice; the nature of his vocation, and his professional, political and social relations, which prepares me to advance a step further in the inquiry, and to endeavor to ascertain the nature of his obligations, liabilities, and duties. As this is not an essay upon the technical liabilities of a lawyer to his client, in damages, for a faithless, ignorant, or negligent discharge of his duty, it is unnecessary to dilate at any length upon this aspect of the subject. At the same time, it is necessary that all of the obligations should be defined and understood.

I use the word "obligations" in a general and somewhat arbitrary sense. I also reverse the natural and logical order of the subject, by considering the "obligations" of lawyers before their "duties." Logically, the "duties" of an individual, or of a class, should be, perhaps, first ascertained, because when a "duty" exists, it generally carries with it a corresponding "obligation," and the violation of an "obligation" involves or creates a "liability."

The obligations which I am now to speak of are well understood by the lawyers. They are his technical legal "obligations" to his client.

These being ascertained and disposed of, I am then in a position to deal with the "duties" of a lawyer to the community, which never have been, or perhaps never can be, enforced in civil or criminal tribunals, existing, as they do, largely *in foro conscientiæ*, but which, nevertheless, constitute the most important attribute of the lawyer's office.

By "obligations" of a lawyer, I mean to include all those of an *enforceable* character; all those "obligations" in which the statutes, decisions, or orders of the Courts have, expressly or impliedly, defined the relations of the lawyers to their clients, and the courts, and have adjudged their violation to create criminal, or civil, liabilities.

There are three classes of these obligations: first, those arising out of acts of professional misconduct, for which he is liable to criminal punishment; second, those acts for which he cannot be proceeded against criminally, but for which he may be disciplined by the courts, acting without the aid of juries, and punished by imprisonment, fine, or the cancellation or suspension of his license to practice; and, third, those for which he may be held liable to the party injured in pecuniary damages. Some of these acts fall under all three heads, others under two, and still others under one. That is to say, a lawyer may be criminally punished, he may have his license revoked, and he may be liable in damages to his offended client for his acts in one transaction. Or, he may not be liable to criminal punishment, but only in damages to his clients, and to the revocation of his license. Or, there may be no damages accrue from his acts, yet, for deceit or misconduct, his license may be revoked.

The first class of obligations, the neglect of which entails a criminal liability, are generally fixed by statute. For instance, in the State of New York, an attorney or counselor who is guilty of any *deceit* or *collusion*, or consents to any *deceit* or *collusion*, with intent to *deceive* the *court* or a *party*, in addition to forfeiting treble damages to the party deceived, is guilty of a misdemeanor.[1] So an attorney buying a bond, etc., or thing in action, with the intent, and for the purpose of bringing an action thereon, is guilty of a misdemeanor.[2]

In these two enactments, the policy of the law

---

[1] Code, Sec. 70.   [2] Code, Sec. 73.

is plainly pronounced, against deceits or collusions of attorneys, and against the practice of buying claims, of any kind, with the purpose of bringing suits thereon.

What constitutes deceit or collusion, *with* intent to *deceive the Court, or a party,* is a question of fact, depending upon the peculiar circumstances of each case. These are difficult offenses to prove. Deceit lurks in the heart, and collusion always is very subtly arranged; and it is only when the fraudulent intent is brought to the surface, and plainly revealed by acts, that the law can be applied. A lawyer who deliberately sits down to concoct or commit a fraud, can hide his tracks, so effectually, in the boundless region of professional discretion, duty, or license, that it is difficult to detect them. But the first of the Statutes to which I have alluded is a very important law, yet to the credit of the Bar, an inactive one.

It is unnecessary to cite any more statutes of a penal nature. They are spread upon the Penal and Civil Codes, and the lawyers, young and old, know them.

The second class of the lawyer's obligations, however, for the violation of which he may be disciplined by the courts, and punished by imprisonment, fine, or the cancellation or suspension of his license to practice, deserves more than a passing notice. Such acts comprehend, in general, everything which a lawyer does, or omits to do, in violation of his duty towards, or in fraud or deceit of, his client, or of the court; or of any contumelious conduct in disobedience or contempt of the latter.

These obligations are not generally defined by statutes, or rules of court; but they exist almost wholly in judicial discretion—in the conscience of the courts.

The Bar seems to comprehend these offenses by a species of intuition, for they embrace all acts of bad faith, and moral misconduct, of the lawyers, in their dealings with their clients, or between themselves.

It is important to note, that many acts which would not subject any other class, of fiduciary agents, to summary punishment, in the case of lawyers, in their dealings with their clients, have been held sufficient to justify the infliction of severe penalties.

It is a principle of universal jurisprudence, that lawyers in their dealings with their clients, and with the court, must observe the strictest rules of honor, fidelity, respect, and obedience. They are held, therefore, to a standard of morals, above and not below the average; a proof that their morale at some time, and in some way, was fixed at a level with their presumed attainments, and corresponding to their opportunities.

Popularly, this is always lost sight of, when a member of the profession incurs censure.

No one has ever successfully attempted, to question the plenary power of the courts, to punish or discipline the lawyers, for any act which they adjudge fraudulent, deceitful, disingenuous, or contemptuous.

This extraordinary power of the courts, summarily, to punish lawyers, by imprisonment, fine, or to deprive them of their licenses to practice law, without a trial and conviction by jury, is put by judges on the ground that lawyers are officers of the court, and that to inspire and maintain a respect for the law, they must exercise a plenary, summary, and almost arbitrary, power over these legal agents.

Although the original ground upon which it is placed, as I have more than once intimated, now exists more in theory than in practice, the power to discipline is unquestionable.

The spectacle of a lawyer acting *amicus curiæ* is now altogether novel, and will soon disappear from sight.

However, the courts, clinging to the old theory, that he is an officer, judge him without mercy or stint, when his professional conduct becomes the subject of judicial review. Indeed, the discipline is so severe, that when a lawyer's conduct comes to be questioned, he is under a positive disadvantage, from the sensitiveness which the judges display to maintain a high standard of professional conduct.

But the number of cases which arise under this second class of obligations, it must be said to the honor and credit of the profession everywhere, when compared with breaches of trust by other fiduciary agents, is not large; and it is not a common sight, to witness the spectacle of a lawyer, (especially one of any character or prominence) arraigned in court, at the instance of a client.

It speaks volumes, for the fidelity of a lawyer to his client and his interests.

The one saving attribute for the lawyer, and through him of society, is *fidelity to the client*. Fidelity is the saving salt of human nature, and ennobles whatever it touches. Subject to the limitations which I recur to hereafter, when discussing his "duties," [1] no risk is incurred to the lawyer's morale by its exercise, and its advantages are incalculable.

It is not the exception, but the rule, for the lawyer to surrender his whole mental, intellectual, and physical power to his client's cause. There are no sacrifices which he will not make, and no dangers that he will not incur, to advance the success of his employment.

[1] Post, p. 124.

Hence the lawyer is not often cited to answer the complaints or grievances of his client; and when such cases arise, they are generally accusations of withholding moneys, or disputes as to compensation, in all of which instances, the strict rules above referred to are enforced.

Little, therefore, can be found, in the history of these infrequent controversies, which throws light upon the duties of a lawyer to the State.

Men do not often publicly complain of the overzealousness of their servants; they do not arraign them for extra fidelity to their interests, and the clients are silent, even when the lawyers overstep all decent, moral, and legal limits, in their efforts for success.

The third class of the lawyer's obligations, for the violation of which he can be made liable to the party injured, in pecuniary damages, is of little importance in this discussion.

As I have said, the violation of an obligation creates a liability, and the lawyer is under a common-law duty in respect to his employment, the same as other agents and trustees.

The lawyer is bound to exercise honesty, skill, prudence, and care, in the management of all business committed to his hands, and his failure to do so subjects him to the ordinary action for damages, at the instance of his client.

The illustrations of this general principle are

to be found in many cases, in which their common-law duties have been defined by the courts,
and they have been sufficiently numerous, to
justify the publication of treatises, devoted especially to that subject.

The consideration of the above three classes
of obligations, is a necessary prologue to the important theme, of the lawyer's real relations and
duties to the State, now so undefined, obscure,
and misunderstood, which I shall proceed to discuss, in the hope that I shall at least open to the
profession, some of the difficult and delicate questions involved in the subject.

CHAPTER IX.

THE "DUTIES" OF A LAWYER.

A "DUTY" in the sense in which I am now considering the subject is, generally, the obligation to perform or exercise the functions of an office in accordance with the nature thereof.

The general duty of a lawyer is, to perform and exercise the functions of his office, in accordance with its nature.

To ascertain this duty, one must understand the true nature of the office. We speak of the duty of a sheriff, of a constable, policeman, executor, or agent. To ascertain their several duties, we must know the character of their functions and of their powers.

I come now to encounter the most difficult, and delicate part of my task,—to draw a line,—between the duty of the lawyer to his client and the State, and another between his conscience and his client, in those matters where to act for his client is a conscious wrong to the community, or to the rights of those to whom he is opposed. Between these lines lay the whole power

124

and influence of the lawyer for good or for evil. Living up to the most exact standards of professional conduct and ethics, the affairs of business and commerce, the ordinary conditions of society, still remain, always opening to the Bar enormous returns in money, reputation, and influence.

While no one can hope, that the lawyers, as a class, will live up to the exact and best models of duty, it is well to have the lines constantly before the profession, so that they can realize how near, or far, they are from ideal conditions. It must be remembered that the profession of the law is necessarily one where an almost boundless discretion is vested in its members. In its general exercise, in the commencement and conduct of litigated or other legal matters, the lawyer has the supreme power of direction. It lies with him to suggest and to direct. There is no arbiter over him, but his conscience. In a very extensive search into the subject, I have found that there has always been a recognized temptation, or tendency, on the part of the lawyers, to overleap the bounds of conscience, and that these acts have frequently called for very stringent measures against them. For example, in 1237, as Matthew Paris informs us, and gives us the text, the Papal Legate in the Great Council held at London in that year, in the extensive pronunciamento which he issued, and which was intended to cover all of the evils of the age, included a separate decree against lawyers, in the following language:

"We have heard the cry of Justice, complaining that it is greatly impeded by the quibbles and cunning of advocates. . . . We therefore, rising to the assistance of Justice, do, with the approbation of the council, decree, that whoever wishes to obtain the office of advocate shall make oath to the diocesan in whose jurisdiction he lives, that in cases in which he may plead, he will plead faithfully not to delay Justice, *or to deprive the other party of it;* but to defend his client both according to law and reason. . . . Let all advocates beware that they do not themselves, or by means of others, suborn witnesses, or instruct the parties to give false evidence, *or to suppress the truth;* those who do so shall be, *ipso facto,* suspended from office and benefice until they have made proper atonement for the same; and if they are convicted for so doing, they shall be duly punished, all other matters notwithstanding."

The duty of a lawyer is threefold:—to the State, as an officer and citizen; to the court, as an officer and adviser; and to his client, as a fiduciary.

He owes loyalty to the State, both as a citizen and as a sworn officer of justice; he owes respect and dignity in his deportment, to the courts, and candor or honesty in his statements and dealings with them; to his client he owes his talents, his knowledge, his time, and his fidelity.

But it is impossible to separate this threefold duty. It cannot be divided into parts. It is like the Trinity, one complete, congruous, whole.

The lawyer cannot perform his duty to one of these parties, and neglect the other two, any more than he can serve two, and neglect the third. He cannot be honest to the State, and dishonest to the court and his client, any more than he can be dishonest to the State and court, and honest to his client.

In every employment which the lawyer receives, his primary duty is to the State. In performing this duty, he can fulfill all of his obligations to clients and courts with fidelity and honor. If he attempts to go beyond this, he strikes a blow at society. Why? Because he is a part of the judicial system of the Government. He is appointed to conduct judicial proceedings. If a conflict arise between his duty to the Government and his Client, in which the position of the State in its whole corporate capacity is clear (not a mere question of law, applicable to both, or a question of the rights of the citizens, which is in fact the interest of the State itself), he must decide in favor of the former, for the interest of that client is subordinate to the interests of all the other citizens—constituting the State—who are interested in maintaining the integrity of the judicial system. *Salus populi suprema lex.* His oath to maintain the laws, cannot be performed by giving advice, or resorting to acts, which cause their violation. Of course, he should not prejudge, and in cases of doubt he is free to act as his conscience dictates,—*honest* doubt as to the law, or *honest* doubt as to the facts.

Suppose constables and policemen receive bribes from criminals to allow them to commit crimes or to escape! Suppose magistrates and judges receive bribes to allow criminals to go unpunished!

Everybody understands and appreciates the effects of such acts, and all agree that a proper punishment should be meted out therefor.

Yet how are these offenses worse than the conduct of lawyers who, knowingly and deliberately, sell their office, influence, and knowledge, to aid or abet clients to take undue advantage of the law? The former can be punished because the acts are capable of proof, but the latter go unpunished because, sheltered in the breast of the lawyer, there is no adequate legal evidence. Is the one class of acts any less dishonest and lawless than the other?

Policemen, constables, magistrates, lawyers, each and all, are parts of the judicial system.

To bribe a policeman to shut his eyes while crime is being committed; to corrupt a magistrate to permit a criminal to escape; to pay a lawyer to use his knowledge to defeat the law; what difference is there in these acts? Is the lawyer's conduct less serious because it is hidden and secret? The law is defeated, somebody is wronged, and the occupation of the lawyer degraded. The difference is not in the degree of the act, but in the difficulty of detection. When a lawyer cheats the law, the act is so insidious that it is almost undiscoverable. He works under the guise of his employment, which is protected all over by the sacred armor of the legal principle, that his dealings with his client are confidential, so confidential that he not only cannot be made to disclose what takes place between them, but he is absolutely prohibited from doing so. Therefore he works with perfect impunity. He is alone with his conscience. The client is not apt to disclose a secret, or plot, which is made for his own benefit, and the disclosure of which would result in getting him into difficulty. The lawyer, therefore, can arrange carefully and delicately the game which his client is to play, to defeat the law—and when the job is "put up" he can go into court, represent his client, place the whole business upon the latter's shoulders, and wrest from justice and the law,

I

results to which the client is not entitled. In the performance of this work, the lawyer artfully puts forward the client. He insidiously fills the latter with false pleas and defenses, and he appears merely as the *representative*, whereas, in fact, he is often the *principal actor*. Is not this pure and simple dishonesty, and is not the lawyer as corrupt as any other officer who takes a direct bribe?

And it is immaterial if the lawyer concocts the scheme, or knowingly aids the client in carrying his own plans into execution. In the one or the other, case, he is equally culpable.

I am bound to say, that the tendency of the lawyer, in modern times, is to look to, and think of, nothing else but the client's interests, and the question as to how far his professional conduct affects the administration of justice, and the general salutary condition of the State, is almost lost sight of—indeed, few lawyers have ever taken time to analyze their true relations in this respect. They are satisfied if the client is successful, and the general damage which such success may have worked, to the law and society, is rarely regarded by them.

It may also be safely said that the prevailing popular idea of the lawyer, too often justified by facts, is, that his profession consists in *thwarting* the law instead of *enforcing* it. The modern idea of a great lawyer is one who can most successfully *manipulate* the law and the facts.   The public no longer calls them "great," but "successful" lawyers.   Not a great jurist, or profound student, but a successful practitioner.   In casting about for legal aid, one constantly hears such phrases as these: "Whom shall we pick out to break, defeat, or thwart this law?"   "Go to Smith; he is very clever and cunning and will get you out of any difficulty."   "Lawyer Jones is your man; he can hoodwink the court and fool the jury."   "Brown has great influence with the court; employ him."   "Do you want time and delay I know the man for you." Availability is sought for—not great legal talent or learning.   And the rights of the public!   They are never thought of, much less considered.   The lawyer goes with the current—the more desperate the causes he wins, the greater his reputation. When he is at the zenith of his professional fame, he can accept the flimsiest case with impunity, and wrangle and wrestle it through the courts, relying upon his past record, and, of course, wholly indifferent to, or unconscious of, the interests of law and of justice.

It is the common belief, inside and outside of the profession, that the most brilliant and learned of the lawyers are employed to defeat or strangle justice.   If a citizen gets into criminal trouble;

if he wishes to postpone paying his debts; if he desires to enforce an illegal demand; if he wishes to defeat a statute, or the policy of the law, he makes choice (according to the magnitude and delicacy of the questions involved, and of his means), of the lowest "shyster" or the most skillful counsel. In some instances, his necessities call for a pettifogger, whose capital stock consists of cunning and impudence, who falsely brags of his intimacy with judges, and his ability to postpone and delay; or, one whose force consists in making flimsy assaults through processes of the law; or a braggadocio with a brazen countenance and loud voice; in others, the dishonest litigant needs the services of a counselor—who stands well socially and politically, but who sometimes has not even a fair power of presentation.

It is believed that big fees will command the leaders of the bar everywhere. It is as well known as any other public fact, that the lawyers of all classes can be hired by the first comer, in any kind of a case, good, bad, or indifferent.

In this view, every lawyer might be regarded as an intellectual prostitute, whose mind, whose time, whose experience, knowledge, and influence can be hired, and occupied, by any stranger, who desires to comply with his terms, as to fees.

A successful lawyer, as thus understood, must necessarily be guilty in the course of his practice, of many dishonorable and disloyal acts to the State, unconsciously sometimes, but often willfully.

If he be a man of fair natural, moral sense, or intuition, he must suffer some qualms of conscience, but by degrees these wear off—for it is the hand of little employment that hath the daintier sense—and he begins to regard it as his duty to accept all of the cases which are proffered to him. His acumen is sharpened, his devices become more numerous, and in time he begins to regard, with feelings of real triumph, the victories which he wrests from the law, at the sacrifice of justice and right. It is his highest glory to be able to say, "I *won* that case," and his air is more triumphant if it is a very bad one. There is nothing secret, or underhand, about this part of the lawyer's business. It has the approval of the people everywhere. No one has ever, successfully, assailed the right of a lawyer to accept a retainer and employment from *any* man, in *any* case. The flimsiest defenses, or pleas, are interposed by the leading lawyers—not by those in the middle rank of the profession.

In fact, the community looks with perfect complacency and composure upon a transaction in which the leading lawyer sells his talent, his knowledge, his time and influence, to the most corrupt or infamous individual in the land; to promote or sustain illegal acts, civil or criminal; while, at the same time, condemning in the most unmeasured terms the client and his performances; condemning the author and his acts, and applauding the lawyer who shields and sustains him! To-day a multi-millionaire, can take his pick of the Bar, in any case.

All these anomalies in law practice, these paradoxes in morals, are constantly witnessed.

Yet if one contemplates the true position which the lawyer fills in the Government, as an auxiliary in the administration of justice, the evil that must result to society, when he transforms himself into an agent, for defeating the object which he is created to promote, becomes apparent. *The idea of the Government licensing an army of legal agents to defeat or delay justice, the exact dispensation of which, is among the first purposes, for which society is organized, is most extraordinary and anomalous.* Remember what I have said about cases in which there is an honest doubt as to the facts, or the law—bear in mind, also in this connection, the right of everyone to insist upon the exact forms and principles of the law being applied. To such cases I do not refer. I allude to those instances in which there is no doubt, where the lawyer is deliberately made an instrument to thwart the law and justice— *and he knows it.*

So those qualities of fidelity to, and sacrifices for, the client, of which I have heretofore spoken, and which are so often illustrated by lawyers in their employment, and which, in the abstract, are virtues highly to be extolled, are no longer virtues, but become positive vices.

Let me not be misunderstood. I would not abate one jot of a noble enthusiasm sustained by one of the best principles of human nature—that of fidelity—in those cases where it can in any wise have a proper application. But surely there are mistakes and excesses here, as in everything else, that is good. A bad cause has had its votaries, and blind attachment to the persons of individuals has ended in ruin and even criminality. Fatuous fidelity has no merit, taking it at its best. When it claims exceptional privileges, as in the case of the lawyer, it should be more closely scrutinized, for it then accompanies a grave function and is encompassed by many-sided duties. Who can doubt that it should then be safeguarded by an *enlightened conscience?* When it is so guarded, there is in reality no choice of evils, no infidelity either to the client or the State, for the duty to the State begins at the point where the duty to the client ceases, and both being bound up with each other, and presumably of equally vital necessity, they serve, in the mind of the advocate, mutually to illustrate each other. A determination, therefore, on the part of the advocate, to devote himself at all hazards to the rescue of his client at the expense of the Law, and, it may be, of truth, can have no vindication from the assumption that it is required by the principle of fidelity. It is, rather, subversive of that principle, rightly understood. Its evil effects, private and public, need no amplification. They are with us, and around us, in plentiful measure.

The lawyer's duty to his client is, to be honest, faithful, skillful, and diligent, and he owes and can justly give him nothing more. If his zeal, cupidity for money, or desire for success or notoriety, pushes him farther, he immediately encroaches upon his duty to the court and the State, and perverts and corrupts the administration of justice. If, in the actual working of any system of jurisprudence, a condition of things exists in which fidelity to the client and the duty to the court, to the law and society, are in opposition to each other, then it is a sure sign that the whole of that state of things, system, courts, lawyers, and public opinion, needs revising.

The lawyer's duty to society and the law must be constantly kept before him, for, while a single act, or all of the acts, of one lawyer may not be enough to affect the foundations of justice, the combined acts of a body of lawyers oft repeated, like an army of worms, silently and secretly gnawing at the foundation of a great and magnificent structure, will gradually but surely cause it to give way and tumble into ruins. It is perhaps not going too far to assert that the lawyers, as a class, are largely answerable, for the minimum of respect and obedience, which the public has for the law. Atlas had not a greater burden on his shoulders, than the responsibilities of the lawyer in this regard.

One may not be able to trace the effect of a single, or of a thousand, dishonest and illegal practices of lawyers, upon the judicial system, but if the wheels of justice become deflected, or the law paralyzed, you may be sure that such acts have contributed largely to the result.

Let anyone consider the effect of forty or fifty thousand legal agents spending their lives in distorting and prostituting the forms of justice, misapplying and perverting its principles, undermining the constitution and laws, and he can make fairly accurate calculations as to the longevity, of the system of government, under which they exist and thrive.

If the philosopher or critic is looking for evidence of decay, let him carefully examine the methods of practice, and the moral and intellectual condition, of the legal profession—especially in this republican form of government, where the influence of the lawyer is so potent for good or for evil—and where in fact, every branch of government, is dominated and administered by him.

The general definition of duty, which I have heretofore given, is sufficient, generally, to expose to the lawyers, the just and proper limits of their office.

The effort to cause them to follow and adhere to a strict line of duty, as thus laid down, is neither visionary nor impracticable. But I have now reached a branch of the discussion where the utmost delicacy, thought, and judgment must be exercised in its treatment. In applying these general principles to particular cases, a vast area of debatable ground is opened, wherein many distinguished, and honest, men have, and may, disagree. It is impossible to state any proposition concerning these duties, without conceding that it is subject to numerous exceptions and conditions. The whole question rests largely, in an intelligent and awakened conscience, of the lawyer himself.

But a satisfactory conclusion may be reached, by keeping, in constant view, the true functions of members of the Bar, and the exact nature of the office which they fill, as I have heretofore endeavored to portray it.

If the lawyers comprehend these things; if a
system of education is introduced, which brings
before them a clear conception of their position
in the government under which they live; if their
consciences are educated and thus quickened;
if the cultivation of a high moral sense is made a
distinctive feature of their education, a different
class of lawyers would soon appear, and many
evils would gradually disappear.

As I have intimated, a review of the history
of lawyers from their origin, shows, that the legislators and the courts have not been unmindful
of the constant temptation to this class, to wan-
der away from a strict line of duty, and to either
openly, or insidiously and secretly, commit many
wrongs in behalf of their clients. The profession of the law holds out a perpetual temptation
to human weaknesses.

The oaths administered to lawyers, upon their
admission, while far from being full and exact,
show that it has always been recognized, that the
lawyers possessed opportunities, to delay, illegally,
the course of justice, by the interposition of frivo-
lous, fraudulent, and unfounded defenses, and to
resort to, and use, many other deceitful and dishonest practices and schemes, to thwart and defeat just claims and demands.

These practices have varied, according to the
exigencies of their clients, or the conditions of

the times. But they have grown so general and open, that they have almost come to be recognized as a legitimate part of the lawyer's functions.

Suitors of all kinds have freely availed themselves of the opportunities to delay, or avoid, the payment of their just debts; and public opinion has not only not closed its eyes to these things, but it has openly encouraged, or approved, them.

It is, therefore, not surprising, that in the course of a research into these subjects, we find that arguments have frequently been put forth, with great solemnity and earnestness, to sustain the lawyers in practices which were openly and flagrantly dishonest, and about which it would seem that no two just persons could disagree. And this criticism is not only applicable to contemporaneous history. For instance, as showing that the lawyers were in some respects no better in ancient days than they are at the present time, it was gravely debated in the sixteenth century between the Doctor and Student: 1st, Whether a lawyer, who knew the right and legitimate heir of a property, was justified in concealing that fact and of investing another, who had no claim whatever to it, with the title to the estate; and, 2d, Whether if a lawyer knew, and had the evidence, of the payment of a debt, he was justified in concealing his knowledge, and collecting the money a second time![1]

The Doctor, happily for the age, was an honest man, and had no difficulty in reaching a conscientious and righteous conclusion in the premises.

But there have been, since that time, frequent discussions among lawyers and others, upon questions of legal ethics, which seem to be equally as plain and simple in their solution, by the application of the principles of common honesty, as those to which I have referred above. None more glaring can be cited than the sentiments laid down by Lord Brougham, in his defense of Queen Caroline, which have done incalculable harm and damage to youthful, designing, or resourceful lawyers. In that celebrated trial, he said:

> "I once before took occasion to remind your Lordships, which was unnecessary, but there are many who may be needful to remind, that an advocate by the sacred duty which he owes his Client, knows in the discharge of that office but one person in the world, *that Client and none other*. To save that Client by all expedient means, to protect that Client at all hazards and costs to all others, and among others to himself, is the

[1] "Doctor and Student," Dialogue I, Chap. XV; Dialogue II, Chap. VI; Dialogue I, Chap. XII.

highest and most unquestioned of his duties; and he must not regard the alarm, the suffering, the torment, the destruction which he may bring *upon any other*. Nay, separating even the duties of a parent from those of an advocate, and casting them, if need be, to the wind, *he must go on reckless of the consequences, if his fate it should unhappily be to involve his country in confusion for his Client's protection*."

I heard a lawyer use this quotation in the defense of William M. Tweed—and then, to make "Ossa like a wart," he piteously added, "I have learned to love William M. Tweed!"—which perhaps he might properly have done, but he need not have used Brougham, and his love together.

There perhaps never was language written, or spoken, which contained worse doctrine than that which I have just quoted, of Brougham, and yet it has been relied on over and over again by lawyers, to cover all kinds of dishonest practices and defenses, and the great name of Lord Brougham is still used, to sustain many ridiculous and false positions of advocates, despite the fact that, as far back as 1859, the author of those destructive and unfounded views, in a letter to Mr. Forsyth,[1] publicly repudiated them by saying that they were used as a sort of political

[1] Forsyth's "History of Lawyers," p. 380, Ed. 1875.

menace. A better defense might be, that it was the exaggeration of an impassioned advocate, defending an innocent woman whose situation called for the utmost sympathy of chivalric natures. But in any rational view it was wholly, unmitigatedly, and disastrously bad. In the discussion which ensued, men like Coleridge, whose opinion I quote,[1] had no difficulty in discerning the proper limitations; but it exactly suited the caliber of those who were to profit by it, and it has stuck like a burr to the profession ever since. And Macaulay, in his Essay on Bacon, left it to his readers to say:

> "Whether it be right that a man should, with a wig on his head, and a band round his neck do for a guinea, what without those appendages, he would think it wicked and infamous to do for an empire; whether it be right that, not merely believing, but knowing a statement to be true, he should do all that can be done by sophistry, by rhetoric, by solemn asseveration, by indignant exclamation, by gesture, by play of

[1] "Table Talk," Oct. 27, 1831: "There is undoubtedly a limit to the exertions of an advocate for his client. He has a right, it is his bounden duty, to do everything which his client might honestly do, and to do it with all the effect which any exercise of skill, talent or knowledge of his own may be able to produce. But the advocate has no right, nor is it his duty to do that for his client which his client *in foro conscientiæ* has no right to do for himself; as, for a gross example, to put in evidence a forged deed or will knowing it to be so forged."

> features, by terrifying one honest witness,
> by perplexing another, to cause a jury to
> think that statement false."

I deem it, therefore, important to specify
some of those acts, which I think must be conceded to be clear violations of the lawyer's
duty, leaving other acts, or courses of professional conduct, to be governed by the general
principles which I have endeavored heretofore to
state:

> (a) To knowingly commence suits for the
> recovery of unjust and unfounded claims;
> or to continue their prosecution, when they
> are discovered to be false and without foun-
> dation in fact.

As an act of this kind involves pure dishonesty,
it would seem to be only necessary to state it,
to prove it. And yet even so pure a man as
Judge Sharswood,[1] unintentionally, throws doubt
upon the subject, by asserting that the lawyer
"is not morally responsible for the act of the
party in maintaining an unjust cause," and that
"when he (the lawyer) has once embarked in a
case, he cannot retire from it, without the consent
of his client or the approbation of the court."

No sophistry can obscure such a position as
being wholly against the common principles of

---

[1] Legal Ethics, pp. 83, 84, 85.

honesty, and the true nature of the lawyer's office.

And Sharswood corrected whatever unfavorable inference might be drawn from the above remarks, by clearly affirming, in a subsequent part of his book [1] that "Counsel has an undoubted right, and are in duty bound to refuse to be concerned for a plaintiff in the legal pursuit of a demand which offends his sense of what is just and right."

The object in creating courts was to administer justice. How, then, can one of the principal sworn agents of the law be justified in knowingly aiding and abetting unfounded and dishonest suits? Upon what principle can he use the machinery of the law to accomplish results contrary to justice, truth, right? How can the law be efficacious, if it is slaughtered in the temple of justice, by its own chosen guards? What is to become of the sanctuary when the priest turns atheist?

A lawyer, with knowledge of the facts, is "morally responsible" for the act of a party in maintaining an unjust cause, because he is willfully stabbing justice, and aiding in the "injuria," which it is the object of all law to prevent or remedy.

If anything can be more distinctly immoral, I cannot conceive it.

[1] Ibid. p. 96.

J

There may be some room for a question, as to the form and method which a lawyer should adopt in retiring from a case which he discovers to be dishonest, but that he should desert it, at once, upon the acquisition of the knowledge, is perfectly clear.

By existing rules of law, a lawyer is forbidden to betray the secrets which come to him under guise of professional confidence; and he cannot, perhaps, walk into court and loudly proclaim the dishonesty of his client,—but there is always an easy avenue of escape from such a situation, without violating the privilege above referred to, and there is no real excuse for not promptly abandoning such a cause. A man who is conducting a dishonest case, should feel no disappointment in failing to secure legal assistance, to help him cheat justice; and frequent rebukes of this kind, from the Bar, would have a quick and exhilarating effect, upon the morals of the litigating community.

If a layman combines with, or assists, his friend, or business associate, in defrauding another of his rights or property, the world has never altered its views as to the nature of the act, and of its entire and unmitigated immorality. And the lawyer, in aiding his client to do the same kind of an act, is guilty of a deeper and more striking offense—because, in addition to the innate immorality of his conduct, he violates his oath and duty as an officer of the law.

Many apposite quotations could be cited from the writings of moralists to sustain these views,[1] but I deem them superfluous, for I believe the subject is perfectly clear, when the true character of the lawyer is understood and considered.

They are, however, strikingly confirmed by the oath of office administered to an Avocat in France, which requires him "de refuser les causes dont il connaitrait l'iniquite." [2]

(b) To knowingly postpone, delay, or defeat, just and legal claims or demands.

This is one of the besetting sins of modern legal practice; but perhaps it is not more so in degree now than in the past. Legal controversies, however, have increased to such enormous proportions that there is little doubt but that such a practice, openly indulged in, talked about, and encouraged, has a direct and deep influence upon the morals of the lawyers, and upon society in general. When the laws can be easily thwarted, the moral sense of the whole community is deadened.

It has almost come to be a proverb in the

---

[1] See especially Whewell, "Elements of Morality," b. II, c. XV, S. 303.

[2] "Usages et Regles de la Profession d'Avocat," etc., par M. Cresson, Vol. I, p. 17.

law—at all events, it is the general open boast of lawyers—that any just and legal claim, may be almost indefinitely postponed, by a resort to technical and dishonest defenses and excuses. There is hardly a lawyer who has not felt justified, at some step of his career, in resorting to such practices.

And yet, when the subject is examined even in the most narrow light of the lawyer's functions and duties, it becomes perfectly plain that these practices, of defending or postponing just and legal claims, must inevitably be to the detriment of the principles of the law and justice. The demoralization which is produced, is as great as the violation of any other plain duty.

Sharswood dwells upon one aspect of this subject in the following language:

> "A man comes to him (his lawyer) and says: 'I have no defense to this claim, it is just and due, but I have not the means to pay it; I want all the time you can get for me.'"[1]

This, no doubt, presents an every-day picture, in the life of a lawyer, and sometimes the deepest consequences to friends, family, and future prospects, are involved in it. The appeal comes to the lawyers, often, in a form which is almost irresistible.

[1] Legal Ethics, p. 116.

Judge Sharswood evidently felt the delicacy of the question, and he meets it by ingenuously saying that, in such a case, an application should be made to the plaintiff for time! But, appreciating the prompt refusal which generally results from such application after suits have been instituted, he says: "If, however, that be impracticable, *it would seem that a suitor has a right to all the delay, which is incident to the ordinary course of justice.* The counsel may take all means for this purpose which do not involve artifice or falsehood in himself or the party." (p. 116) ". . . *The formal pleas put in are not to be considered as false in this aspect,* except such as are required to be sustained by oath."

Of course, when Sharswood wrote his little book, Pennsylvania existed under a pure common-law practice, and the declarations and pleas were not under oath. But that circumstance does not alter the principle, which I am here discussing.

There is no doubt, that many lawyers have received encouragement, in the practice of interposing technical defenses, to just claims, from arguments or reasoning of this kind, and it has made the practice more common and extended. The difficulty is that, by the abandonment of the lawyer's plain field of duty, consequences ensue which are disastrous to the proper administration of justice.

The plaintiff, or owner of an undisputed claim, has rights. He is entitled to have them vindicated, when they are refused, or disregarded, and the courts are established for that purpose. If these rights are postponed or defeated, the consequences may be as disastrous to the claimant as to the debtor. Where is the line to be drawn? Certainly not between the formal pleas not under oath, and those which are attested by an affidavit.

The one is equally as false as the other, and in this aspect the form of the defense, if unsupported by merit, is equally objectionable in conscience and truth.

There is no act which has brought upon the administration of the law more reproach, if not contempt, than these unrighteous and unjustifiable delays, procured by attorneys, for necessitous and dishonest suitors.

Individuals frequently abandon their legal rights, rather than embark upon the doubtful voyage of a litigation, which may end in the far future, and involve such expense, annoyance, and trouble as substantially amount to a loss of their claims.

"Go to law and lose it all;" "go to law and be involved in endless litigation and expense;" "give it to the lawyers and be done with it;" are expressions that are familiar to everyone.

The "law's delay" has been proverbial, in English history, from time immemorial, but its origin and continuation, were based upon grounds, very different from those which are now invoked to support it. So far as I can discover, these delays were to a considerable extent the result of the intricacies and forms of pleadings, and the respect paid to them by the lawyers and the courts, and without doubt many dishonest suitors sought refuge for time, and procured postponements under their cover. In Chancery proceedings the delays were cruelly long and unjust, and *Jarndyce* v. *Jarndyce*, is not an exaggerated illustration of them. It may be conceded, that the general tendency of modern times, has been towards greater rapidity, in the transaction of legal, as well as other, business, but the criticism of delays predicated upon false and dishonest defenses is not answered by a recourse to the past. These delays constitute to-day a crying, open, wholesale, shameful reproach upon justice, which threatens the very fabric of jurisprudence. A hardly appreciable evil, which, in Shakespeare's age, was sufficient to attract that great poet's satire, has now grown to such dimensions, as to involve all of the legal agents, and the administration of justice itself—it is applicable to a whole system.

Its danger lies in the fact that it has permeated

all classes of society, and citizens everywhere unblushingly use the lawyers to procure unconscionable delays, and to thwart and defeat the payments of their just debts and demands.

These practices, so evil in themselves, must likewise be dangerous. Whatever corrupts the community, also threatens institutions. In the connection which exists between the Law, and those who are charged with its administration, all that subverts the morale of the latter, must be dangerous to the former, as an instituted organism, and if to one such vital organism, both directly and reflectively, to all.

Before I close under this head I must advert to a most vicious practice of lawyers, in lending the influence of their office, legal ability and experience, to thwart the right of individuals to dispose of their property by will. No more sacred or interesting right grew up with the growth of jurisprudence. The importance of rigidly guarding this power is so apparent that I need not dwell upon it. The rule of permitting an individual to bestow his property upon his death according to the dictates of his will, judgment, or even caprice, grows out of reasons which operate to sustain and make healthy the social organization. It is an incentive to ambition; it invites prudence and economy; it is a powerful weapon for the proper education and discipline of families; it teaches charity, and it generates a respect for law and order.

But the lawyers have rendered this plain principle of law nugatory. Upon feigned, and assumed grounds, they break wills, and frustrate the testator's intention, until the doctrine of testamentary disposition has come to be almost a mockery. No will is safe from their brazen and shameful attacks, and when they are successful, property is wrested from devisees and legatees, and, generally, given to persons whom the testators deliberately, intentionally and expressly desire not to have it. The sacred right becomes nugatory.

(c) A lawyer is not justified in using or resorting to dishonest means or practices in the defense of persons accused of crime.

The question whether an advocate should defend a person for a crime of which he knows, or believes, him to be guilty, has always been a favorite topic for discussion, in, and out of, the legal profession.

I do not intend to avoid the last-named issue by seeking refuge behind this third (c) proposition, which I have just laid down. I believe, however, that the subject, when fully understood, has less practical importance than is generally ascribed to it.

In the outset, it is necessary to clearly define,

what is meant by a "knowledge or belief," of the guilt of the accused person.

If the lawyer has personal knowledge of the crime; if he is present at, or sees, its commission, he is a witness, the same as any layman, and consequently would, for obvious reasons, be practically disqualified from acting as an advocate.

He may also derive his knowledge of a crime, from a voluntary confession, made to him by his client.

In such a dilemma, what is his duty? His mouth is closed by the law, even if he should wish to speak, because the law prevents him from disclosing information, communicated to him in his professional capacity.

Should he continue to act as the advocate in such a case? Nothing can be gained by an endeavor to answer such hypothetical or supposititious questions. They depend, largely, upon the peculiar circumstances of each case, and must be conscientiously determined by the lawyer when they arise. It may be, that there is a full, technical, case against the accused, without his confession—which fact might influence the lawyer as to one course of conduct. On the other hand, there might be a defect in the technical proof against the defendant, which the confession would supply. Should the lawyer advise his client to plead guilty? Suppose he gave such advice and the client refused to follow it? I repeat that each case must be determined as it arises, in view of its peculiar circumstances, keeping in sight the general principles which I shall hereafter, briefly, refer to.

What is, generally, meant, therefore, when the question is asked if a lawyer should defend a person accused of crime whom he "knows *or believes*" to be guilty, is, that his knowledge, or belief, is derived from sources of information which are open to everybody, and upon which men generally form and base their opinions— viz., through the Press, and from current and public report and rumor. No important criminal act is committed, which is not quickly communicated to the public, and about which the community, and lawyers in common, do not, promptly, form an opinion.

With an opinion of guilt, based upon such sources of knowledge and belief, is a lawyer justified in defending the culprit? With this moral conviction of guilt upon his mind, has he the right to espouse such a cause?

I think there can be no grave doubt as to his complete right to do so.

The court certainly can assign counsel, to defend all cases, in which prisoners have none; and their duty, as officers of the court, would compel them to obey such orders.

The right of the lawyer, to defend persons accused of crime, rests upon broad and well-grounded principles. There must necessarily exist in every community, governed by law, exact and clear definitions of crimes, as well as certain forms and rules for the trial of offenders. These are indispensable conditions, to an intelligent, and humane, administration of criminal jurisprudence.

A person accused of crime, is entitled to demand that each, and all, of these conditions, should be satisfied, before he is convicted.

No system of criminal jurisprudence could exist, without such general rules.

While there is no doubt that, at times, the application and enforcement of these forms of criminal procedure, prevent the conviction and punishment of guilty persons, yet, upon their continuance and stability, depend the very existence of social organization.

For instance, a cold and atrocious murder may be committed, the person who committed the bloody deed discovered and arrested; and the mind of the community morally convinced of his absolute guilt; yet if all of the witnesses who had knowledge of it should die, the guilty man would go unpunished. The requirements of the law could not be met, and justice would be thwarted.

A lawyer's right and duty, are, to demand that his client, charged with crime, should be proceeded against in a legal and orderly manner, notwithstanding his own moral conviction of guilt. If the elements constituting the crime charged, are lacking; if the forms of the law are not complied with; it is his duty to urge and demand the acquittal of his client. In doing this, he performs a double duty—one to the community, in preserving and upholding the forms of the law, and the other to his client.

No finer or nobler exhibition of his real duty to the State, can be imagined, than the position of the lawyer, under such circumstances.

As Erskine eloquently, almost passionately, said:

"I will for ever, at all hazards, assert the dignity, independence, and integrity of the English Bar, without which, impartial justice, the most valuable part of the English Constitution, can have no existence. From the moment any advocate can be permitted to say that he will or will not stand between the crown and the subject arraigned in the court where he daily sits to practice, from that moment the liberties of England are at an end. If the advocate refuses to defend, from what he may think of the charge or of the defense, he assumes the character of the judge; nay, he assumes it before the hour of judgment, and in proportion to his rank and reputation, puts the heavy influence of perhaps a mistaken opinion into the scale against the accused, in whose favor the benevolent principle of English law makes all presumptions, and which commands the very judge to be his counsel."

This utterance, as is known, was made in a great public case, yet the principle applies to every case where law can be invoked in behalf of a party. A lawyer can always demand that the forms of the law should be complied with and upheld.

I do not place the right of the lawyer, to defend a client, whom he believes to be guilty, upon the ground that he cannot know that his client is guilty, until his guilt has been officially and finally declared, by a court and jury, because he often does know, in the sense that he has a moral conviction of the guilt of his client, which he has derived, through the ordinary channels of information.

I place the right of the lawyer upon the ground that he is an officer of the law, and that it is his duty to see that the forms of the law are carried out, quite irrespective of individual knowledge.

The argument that the lawyer cannot know of the guilt of his client until he has been officially adjudged so, might be used with equal force by an accessory after the fact. Why could

not every accessory after the fact declare, with
the same reason as the lawyer, that he could not
know that a crime had been committed, because
the person whom he had assisted, had not been
adjudged judicially guilty? In every civilized
government, rules are adopted in the body of
the criminal jurisprudence, to punish, severely,
all persons who aid, or abet, in the commission of
crime, or who, after its commission, aid, or abet,
a criminal to escape detection, capture, or punishment. An accessory before, or after the fact,
is recognized as almost as bad as the principal
criminal.

An accessory after the fact is a person who
knows a felony to have been committed, and who
relieves, comforts, or assists the felon. Therefore, to make an accessory *ex post facto*, it is in
the first place requisite that he knows of the felony
committed. And generally any assistance whatever, given to a felon to hinder his apprehension,
trial or punishment makes the assistor an accessory,—as, furnishing him with a horse to escape
his pursuers, money or victuals to support him,
a house or other shelter to conceal him, or open
force and violence, to rescue or protect him. And
so strict is the law, where a felony is actually
complete, in order to do effectual justice, that
the *nearest relations* are not suffered to aid or
relieve one another. If the parent assists his

child, or the child the parent, if the brother receives the brother, the master his servant, or the servant his master, or even if the husband receives his wife, who have any of them committed a felony, the receivers become accessories *ex post facto*. A married woman, however, does not come within this rule, because she is presumed to act under the coercion of her husband.

We see, therefore, for the maintenance of society, with what strictness and severity, the hand of the law is uplifted against those who aid, or shelter, or assist, criminals to escape their just and necessary punishment.

But the lawyer's duty is not to aid or assist the guilty to escape—although that may be the result of his efforts—but it is to see that the forms of the law are maintained. To do this he can employ his knowledge and experience, and all of the arts of advocacy in his attempts to acquit clients, without a resort to dishonest and covert means and practices.

If these views be correct, it would seem to follow, that the lawyer's duty, to defend a person in those cases where he has a belief, or a moral conviction, of the guilt of his client, is quite clear.

And the community cannot suffer, if he simply confines his efforts to demanding that the forms and rules of the law be carried out.

I do not believe that any real service can be

rendered to the profession by pursuing this line
of thought further; or in considering any more
specific propositions. With a full conception
of the general nature of his duties, it is with the
lawyer himself to determine, whether he will aid,
or defeat, justice. No special rules can be laid
down, for all kinds of conditions constantly con-
front him.

Keeping in view that he is an officer of the
court in the real meaning of the term, that a
court is a place where justice is judicially administered, and the remarks of an eminent Equity
Judge, Lord Langdale,[1] that "lawyers are *min-
isters of justice*, acting in *aid* of the Judge before
whom they practice"—the lawyer cannot go far
astray, in the discharge of his duty.

In the complete performance of the latter, the
lawyer becomes the most useful and important
member of the community—a true patriot of
his country, a faithful and intelligent representative of his client, and a useful officer of the court.

And Christopher St. Germain, the author of
the immortal Dialogues between a Doctor and
a Student, of the Laws of England, nearly four
centuries ago,[2] laid down in beautiful but strong
language, a rule which, if it could be followed,
would give us a race of ideal lawyers at once:

[1] 1 Keen, "Reports in the Rolls Court," p. 659. [2] "Doctor and Student," p. 15.

K

"As a light is set in a lantern, that all that is in the house may be seen thereby, so Almighty God hath set Conscience in the midst of every reasonable soul as a light whereby he may divine and know what he ought to do, and what he ought not to do. Wherefore, forasmuch *as it behoveth thee to be occupied in such things as pertain to the law, it is necessary that thou ever hold a pure and clean conscience.*"

"And I counsel thee, that thou love that which is good, and fly that which is evil; that thou do to another, as thou wouldest should be done to thee; *that thou do nothing against Truth;* that thou do justice to every man as much as in thee is; and also that in every general rule of the law, thou do observe and keep equity. And if thou do thus, I trust the lantern that is in thy conscience shall never be extincted."

But this conscience, which should guide the lawyer, comes of training and education. It is not wholly innate, it doth not spring up spontaneously or by intuition; it is the result of an exact and perfect study and comprehension of the office and duties of a lawyer. It should be made the first, and most important, part of his legal education. Along with, and as part of it, the lawyer is bound by study, self-denial, and genuine hard work, at some time to master the history and science of the Law itself; and then, by a course of liberal reading, he should enlarge his sympathies, and seek to eliminate from his mind all narrow prejudices of nationality, race, and creed; that his standards of men should not be the abuse of the ideal, and run into the impractical and visionary, on the one hand, or the self-asserting, or flippant, on the other; but humane and generous, keeping in view, always, the limits fixed by nature and circumstances. All his powers, otherwise, even when accompanied by mere honesty of purpose, may become the cause of great evils.

To a man so equipped and prepared, the vision of his whole duty, is soon opened to him, in the clearest and fullest sense.

CHAPTER X.

CAUSES AND REMEDIES.

THE seeds of reform are of slow growth. They very rarely produce a full crop in the season in which they are sown. They bear fruit, scatteringly. An old and pernicious system, cannot be extirpated, as one would raze a house, and build a new one in its place. A conspicuously rotten plank may be replaced by a new one, until by degrees the whole edifice is sound. Therefore it would be useless, to attempt to reform, the present generation of lawyers, as a whole, for they are, inextricably, involved in the meshes of codification, and its evil results. The ground can be prepared, now, and new ideas of reform promulgated, which, will take effect upon the next generation, and it can be hoped, that eventually a new race of lawyers will appear, divided into two classes,—Attorneys, or Solicitors, and Counselors, or Barristers.

I proceed now to classify the existing conditions and their causes, and to suggest remedies, which, in my opinion, will essentially mitigate, if not exterminate, existing evils.

164

FIRST: THE FIRST CRITICISM IS THAT THERE ARE GENERAL DEFICIENCIES, IMPERFECTIONS, AND LOOSENESS IN THE PRELIMINARY, ELEMENTARY, AND LEGAL EDUCATION OF LAW STUDENTS.

I. Insufficient educational requirements and examinations preliminary to matriculation as a legal apprentice.

Reform of the law cannot be superficial. It must go to the root of the evil. It must begin at the bottom. It must be contemporaneous with legal apprenticeship.

A person who wishes to study law should possess a real, elementary education, and, in addition to the other necessary qualifications, should know the Latin language and its general literature. He should, also, be able to pass an examination, in one other modern language, preferably Spanish, from our expected future relations with that race. No certificates from colleges, or schools, should be accepted, as proof of these requirements, but each candidate should pass through the ordeal, of an actual examination, under the direction of properly appointed, and qualified, examiners.

II. Deficiencies in education and instruction of law students.

(a) In length of time of legal apprenticeship.

It should be not less than seven years, of which three, should be actually spent, as a clerk, in a law office.

(*b*) Absolute want of instruction, of legal apprentices, in the functions and duties of lawyers, and professional ethics.

(*c*) No, or insufficient, instruction in the primary principles and elements of jurisprudence—foundation, nature, object, and spirit of laws.[1]

(*d*) No instruction in the functions and duties of legislators.

(*e*) No, or inadequate, instruction in American historical, and Federal and State, constitutional, law.

(*f*) No, or insufficient, instruction in criminal jurisprudence, in its origin and purpose, and in the pleadings, evidence, and practice, connected therewith.

It is fashionable to taboo this branch of jurisprudence. It is avoided and shunned as rather disreputable. To say of one "he is a purely criminal lawyer" involves, it is assumed, a certain obloquy; that he does not occupy a first rank in the profession. Notwithstanding this ignorant criticism, it may be confidently asserted, that the study and practice of criminal law, awaken and exercise, the best mental and moral qualities of lawyer, advocate, and citizen. In fine, it is

[1] Columbia College undertakes to fulfill this requirement in one of her courses, and has an able man to perform the function; but the time is too short, and the instruction and attention necessarily superficial.

impossible to conceive of a great civil lawyer, who has not considerable knowledge of criminal law.

(*g*) No, or insufficient, clinical training, in the office of a practicing lawyer.

III. Deficient and non-systematic education in all of the branches of law.

Case law is taught, instead of elementary law. Blackstone, the greatest institutional writer, is practically abolished, from Law Academies and Colleges. There is not a word, in his commentaries, which should be dropped from a legal course.

Requirements of law examining boards are superficial.

In addition to prolonging the apprenticeship to seven years I advocate the following:[1]

1. The abolition of "case" law as a fundamental means of instruction, and the introduction of the study of law from text-books, substantially as follows:

2. The study of institutional law, by a complete mastery of Blackstone's, and Kent's Commentaries, and Walker's American Law.

3. Pleadings, Evidence, and Practice—the

----

[1] Except in a few instances I do not mention the text-books which should be adopted. There are good and bad ones. Most of them are too hastily put together, but a judicious selection can be made by competent lawyers.

latter embracing Federal and State practice, and Equity and Common-Law practice.

4. Natural and civil law, and the principles, foundation, and spirit of law, with such books as the following:

Paley's "Moral and Political Philosophy."
Burlamaqui's "Natural Law."
Montesquieu's "Spirit of Laws."
Puffendorf.
MacIntosh's "Discourses on the Study of the Law of Nature and Nations."

Judicious Selections from Savigny, Pothier, Domat, Grotius, and d'Aguesseau.

5. The law of personal property.

6. The law of real property.

7. The law of contracts.

8. The law of corporations.

9. The law of principal and agent.

10. The domestic relations.

11. Equity Jurisprudence.

12. Constitutional Law, including Federal and State, together with the principles of legislation and the duties of legislators.

13. Criminal Jurisprudence.

14. The law of Executors and Administrators.

15. A course of lectures, study, or education, upon the history and chronology of the law reports. The law student should know the history of the re-

ports, and where, and under what circumstances, they were published or promulgated.[1]

16. The study of selected cases.

This order of legal study is of course arbitrary. The study of the law, under proper tuition, can be made interesting and fresh, and, instead of being a burden, and an effort, it can be converted into a delightful occupation. It depends upon the tuition, and when and how it is commenced and pursued. But, primarily, the study should be begun in a natural way, commencing with the organization of society, and opening up to the student, the logical and historical development of the law.

SECOND: THE EXISTING STATE OF THE LAW AND LAWYERS ARISES, PRINCIPALLY, FROM CODIFICATION, SO CALLED, BY WHICH THE PRACTICE OF THE LAW IS CONCENTRATED UPON FORM, RATHER THAN SUBSTANCE, INVITING AND CREATING WHOLESALE TRICKERY AND SHARP PRACTICES, ALL PRODUCING THREE OF THE WORST ENEMIES OF JUSTICE AND JURISPRUDENCE, I. E., (1) DELAYS, (2) COSTLINESS, AND (3) UNCERTAINTY; TO SAY NOTHING OF ITS BALEFUL INFLUENCE UPON THE LAWYERS.

[1] I have not embraced all of the topics involved in a complete legal education, such as Admiralty and Patent Law; but these, and all of the other subjects omitted, are necessarily encountered by the student in his general reading. They can be specially pursued if desired.

The difference between a common-law lawyer, and the practitioner under the Code, is the difference between a surgeon and a butcher.

Behold the title to the New York Code of Civil Procedure!

> "An Act to *simplify* and *abridge* the *practice, pleadings,* and *proceedings* of the courts of this state!"

How the irony of legal history frowns on this assumptious sentence. The Code has earned its own title; or, perhaps, it would be more truthful to say, it has written its own epitaph. It should be called:

> "An Act to *complicate, multiply, befog,* and *render uncertain* the practice, pleadings, and proceedings of the courts of this State."

The effect of the introduction into American Jurisprudence of ignorant, illogical, and imperfect codification, has been to deprive the practice of law, of all its science, and to change wholly its intellectual grade, or standard.

Among other vain pretensions, the so-called Reformers indulged in the futile, and ignorant, attempt to amalgamate law and equity.[1]

---

[1] Sec. 3339: "There is only one form of civil action. The distinction between actions at law and suits in equity, and the forms of those actions and suits, have been abolished."

At the same time, they carefully preserved, the Courts of Equity, in what were known as Special Terms—where trials were had without a jury. Since the adoption of the Code in 1848, thousands of litigants have received purely equitable relief. Jurisprudence is impracticable, without the separate existence of these two systems. And, forsooth, the distinction between law and equity is abolished in New York!

The effect of modern American codification, has been to divert the student, from a study of the elements and principles of jurisprudence, (as witness the banishment of Blackstone as a whole) upon which the maxims and rules of the law are founded, and to convert him into a disputer of the meaning of statutory language. Instead of seeking the truth, the Courts and the Bar, are engaged in the pursuit of technicality and form. I cannot undertake a full criticism of codification. It would require books as large as the three immense volumes of the New York Annotated Code of Civil Procedure—and these contain *only* 4704 pages of closely printed matter including the index! I only indulge in this single, general, sweeping, statement, that one cannot cast his eye upon any part of the Code, which is not receiving a daily bath, of new interpretation from the courts; or without stumbling upon some gross blunder!

The effort to make the law, and its forms and

practice, an open book to all, has been to lower and cheapen the profession of the lawyer—to throw the law into inextricable confusion and doubt—to entail vast expense upon suitors—to create law libraries filled with worthless books, containing records of disputes upon questions of form and practice—and to substitute these latter and minor considerations for those of substance, justice, and right; and principally, to cause delay and expense in the administration of the law. We have now every one of the evils, complained of, in the old system, without the certainty which had been evolved from it, or its harmonious relations, to the whole of the law, as a science.

The fallacy, of the violent criticism of the forms, of common-law practice and pleading, upon which public sentiment was created, to influence what was, ignorantly, called "law reform," has now been thoroughly exposed and exploded.

We have had in New York nearly sixty years of experience (since 1848) of codification, and the experiment has been a lamentable failure. In money, it has cost millions of dollars to suitors; in practice, it has ruined at least two generations of lawyers—and it will probably ruin two more.

Never, was the system, and technique, of the common law, more completely and handsomely, vindicated. Invoke the thousands of silent witnesses, collected on the shelves of law libraries, in New York, in the shape of legal precedents, which testify that most of the cases, enshrined in the law reports, arose out of mere questions of form and practice.

The forms of the common law, and its practice, may have been the subject of some just criticism, calling for amendment; but, to extirpate a whole system to correct a few evils inseparable in some shape from any system; to cut down and cast out as worthless a whole body of judicial procedure, never arbitrarily imposed, but the well-considered growth of ages of experience, when a few simple amendments would have remedied all redundancies and supplied all deficiencies; to dig up whole, when the pruning knife was all that was needed—was, to my mind, simply the work of barbarians. It came from the impatience of those who, not understanding what they destroyed, found it more easy to destroy than to understand; or who, itching for the title of law reformers, struck a blow at the most prominent feature of the law; or who had an ambition to reform, without the time, or the ability, to accomplish it.

To say nothing of the extra costs and expenses; the manifold delays and intricacies of legal procedure; the attempt to simplify has been to bemuddle, confound, and destroy—to produce a race of pigmy lawyers, chattering and quarreling over the meaning of words, in the Code. The manufacture of artificial diamonds, rubies, and emeralds has attained such a state of perfection, that it is almost impossible to detect their spurious quality, without the magnifying glass, in the hands of an expert. The modern Codes produce artificial or paste lawyers. They shine, sparkle, and blaze at a distance, but when their qualities are put in a proper crucible, they are found not to be of the real quality, or first water. They are put together quickly, and made to shine by false and artificial lights and colors. I am of course speaking as a whole.

The multiplication of precedents, has invited and encourages technical, narrow, illogical, sophistical, and unjust distinctions and arguments, in efforts to defeat real justice.

Codification has prevented the full and perfect development of the intellectual, moral, and forensic qualities of lawyers.

Legal digests, analyses, and encyclopedias of law, practice, and forms, have diverted the legal student, from the study of the elements and principles of jurisprudence, to a search after cases. He has become a mere "case lawyer;" he stops at mere form.

Out of the confusion, doubt, and chaos of codification, there will gradually be formed, a logical and compact system, of legal forms, practice, and procedure, which will closely resemble that of the common law, and after years of experiment we will land exactly at the spot from which we started; that is, if the legal mind, like a way-worn traveler, be not lost in the jungles, and come to some otherwise more evil fate. *Facilis descensus Averni.*

Already there have been, practically, three codifications since 1848. And the codifying fiend, still perseveres, in his devastating work, which, like the ravages of a prairie fire, spreads over the whole system of jurisprudence, leaving everything black and ruined, in its course.

THIRD: THE EXCESSIVE NUMBER OF LAWYERS, IS DETRIMENTAL, BOTH TO THE COMMUNITY AND THE MORALE, OF THE PROFESSION.

It creates, encourages, and continues illegal, unfounded, and fraudulent practices, demands, and litigation, because necessarily many of the lawyers depend, not upon professional knowledge and accomplishments, but upon sharpness and cunning. In the effort to sustain themselves, much unnecessary and unfounded litigation is inaugurated, and many disgraceful practices engendered. For example, how many lawyers' offices does an individual need to visit, to procure an attorney to make a defense to a suit, where there exists no meritorious or substantial answer? Men and women spend days in searching for a peculiar kind of precious stone, or a brooch, or a present. But when an individual wishes a lawyer to interpose a dishonest defense, he will probably not be fatigued in the effort to find him. He will, possibly, not go beyond the first office. And he will encounter the same experience, if he wishes to institute an unfounded, or unjustifiable, action. The lawyers will weave from a mere thread of truth, a whole cause of action, or an entire defense. Cunning and trickery often displace real knowledge and ethics. But do not place all of the blame upon the shoulders of the lawyers. If one sensitively honest lawyer be found, there are dozens of others who will act. Besides, how much of the obloquy should fall upon the clients?

An excessive number of, badly trained, lawyers makes the profession cheap and common—plebeian.

It would follow, naturally, that the introduction of a system, such as I have briefly outlined here, would immediately operate to curtail the number of lawyers.

FOURTH: THE GENERAL LACK OF MANNERS, AND THE ALMOST TOTAL LOSS OF AN *esprit de corps*, AMONG THE MEMBERS OF THE BAR.

The lack of respect for the Judges, as by not

habitually saluting them with uplifted hat; the want of respect for the age and experience of brother lawyers; discourtesies among lawyers, making the practice of the law, like a fight between ruffians, for the possession of plunder. Lack of manners, produces a contempt for each other, and, for the profession, which we follow. As Burke says, "The degree of estimation in which any profession is held becomes the standard of the estimation in which the, professors hold themselves." A good-sized book could be written upon this aspect of the subject.

FIFTH: THE ADVENT OF WEALTH, AS THE SOLE CRITERION, OF ARISTOCRATIC, OR SOCIAL, POSITION AND DISTINCTION, TO THE EXCLUSION OF INTELLECTUALITY, REFINEMENT, AND LITERARY, CULTURE.

It has enabled its possessors to buy, or secure, political and social positions, which should be attained only by real merit, refinement and learning.

This has, undoubtedly, affected the prestige of the legal profession, and deprived its members, of true ambition, and moral influence.

When such a criterion is adopted, it is evident that the ambition to excel by right methods must be crushed; of what use, then, is the formation of character, and of the long and studious vigil?

L

The fact that the profession of politics can secure judicial positions, and professional honors and emoluments, tends in the same direction, and adds a positively corrupting element in the lawyer's ambition. If fame and power, can be obtained through politics, (very soon it will be through politics alone), then, such influence as the profession gives, will be enlisted on the side of politics, and politics, not law, become the aim and end of the lawyer's aspirations.

SIXTH: THE RADICAL CHANGES WHICH HAVE OCCURRED IN ALL PROFESSIONS AND BUSINESS AND COMMERCIAL OCCUPATIONS AND RELATIONS, RESULTING, INTER ALIA, IN THE FOLLOWING:

Changing law into a business.

The institution of incorporated companies and agencies to transact conveyancing and legal business with cheapness and guaranties.

The effect of which has been to deprive the lawyers of a large part of their old business, and to drive them into new, and perhaps more important, fields of practice, where hard common sense, good business judgment and acumen, supplant profound, technical, legal knowledge and ability; where they become associates in business adventures, instead of pure counselors, and where their compensation, is based upon the ultimate outcome, and profits, of the business.

Rendering the study and practice of forensic eloquence, unnecessary and superfluous—nay almost ridiculous.

SEVENTH: THE INCREASE OF LITIGATION HAS CAUSED (PERHAPS, IN JUSTICE TO THE BENCH, I SHOULD SAY "FORCED"), THE ADOPTION BY THE COURTS, OF RULES, WHICH FURTHER LIMIT THE TRUE SCOPE OF THE LAWYER'S FUNCTIONS.

These rules, make the occupation of a lawyer, one of pure commercial business.

They do not so much produce brevity of speech, as they destroy the taste, and render useless the cultivation, of ornate, classic, and finished legal arguments, and all those habits of mind which connect the profession with literature and general knowledge, with all of their elevating and refining influences, tending more and more to degrade the law into a mechanical occupation.

EIGHTH: THE EXISTENCE OF AN UNDEFINED FEELING AND SENTIMENT THAT JUDGES IN CERTAIN LOCALITIES ARE, TO A GREATER OR LESS DEGREE, SUSCEPTIBLE TO POLITICAL, OR OTHER SOCIAL, FRIENDLY, OR EVEN CORRUPT, INFLUENCES IN THE PERFORMANCE OF THEIR DUTIES.

Whatever tends, otherwise, to lower the professional standard, also tends to lay it open to

this imputation. How often we hear these remarks: "What Judge shall we bring this before?"
"Whom shall we select from the Bar to argue
this case before Judge X?" "We cannot argue
this case before Judge X because he is the inti-
mate associate of the plaintiff's or defendant's
counsel," as the case may be? In most instances
this is a cruel and unfounded reflection upon the
judges.

But this sentiment undoubtedly exists in many
of our larger cities. Not necessarily based upon
the physical corruption of the judges (a rare vice),
—there is a moral corruption, equally as bad in its
results upon the judges, the bar and the community.

It makes it appear to the litigants that it is
necessary to select *not* an advocate of a higher
order of intellectual endowments, or legal learning,
but one exercising a supposed moral, or political
influence, upon the mind of the judge—one to
whom, in cases of intricacy or doubt, or where
the question is "close"—when strict, independent,
legal judgment is of the highest importance—
the judge can throw his discretion, or opinion, in
favor of his friends, and without regard to the
harmony of the judicial system.

This is the worst species of corruption—because the judge, free from actual bribery, concealing his judicial discretion in a mist of meta-

physical doubt and false reasoning, awards the judgment, contrary to his inner conscience, and to the real equities of the case.

In litigation involving large and important results, the lawyers who breathe in such an atmosphere, sacrifice their own convictions, stifle their own ability, and resort to means which are more certain of success.

The natural demoralization, which such conditions have upon the bar, can be, readily, appreciated—and the clients and courts do not escape the contagion.

NINTH: THE ENORMOUS EXTENSION OF THE PRACTICE OF CONTINGENT COMPENSATION, HAS UNDOUBTEDLY AFFECTED THE CONDITION OF THE BAR, TO SOME EXTENT. HOW GREAT, IT IS NOT POSSIBLE, EXACTLY, TO SAY.

I refrain from expressing any final opinion upon this subject. It is one of profound importance, as bearing on the morale of the profession, and on the administration of the law. It is also one of great delicacy. The power and wealth of our corporations are so tremendous, that in many instances, without some arrangement between lawyer and client, of a contingent character, it is sure great hardship and wrong would occur, without a possibility of redress. The power and concentrated methods, of these bodies, are almost overwhelming. Without contingent arrangements, with lawyers, their power would become oppressive and tyrannical. But the point is whether the practice of contingent fees has not outgrown all just proportions, and is not the direct cause of much unfounded litigation and blackmail.

The ethical objection, to contingent fees, consists in making the lawyer a party to the suit, and therefore, necessarily, a formulator of litigation, often of a doubtful character. It is, besides, a kind of fraud upon the court, and a perversion and confusion of the mind of the advocate. When the interests of justice, can be subserved, on behalf of a poor, or helpless, client, and when the fee itself in no wise takes advantage of his necessities, such practice generally can be reconciled, with the interests of the community, and with professional honor.

The uncertainty, of the results of an appeal to the law, has increased, with the increase of litigation, and this adds another powerful motive to contingent arrangements.

In those instances, where pure commercial business results are sought for, without litigation, the question of fees is changed into commissions, or divisions of profits, and the lawyer being transferred to a mere agent, the ordinary difficulties which surround the subject, do not prevail.

TENTH: THE NON-EXISTENCE OF A DIVISION OF THE BAR INTO TWO CLASSES: 1ST, ATTORNEYS OR SOLICITORS; AND, 2D, COUNSELORS OR BARRISTERS.

No matter how this question might have been decided many years ago, the vast changes in, and increase of, business, require the profession to be divided into two classes. I have already alluded to this subject.[1] I think I have said that this division would, alone, stop many causeless suits which are now begun.

ELEVENTH: THE LAWYERS SHOULD WEAR A GOWN OR APPROPRIATE BADGE IN COURT.

The fact that lawyers do not wear a distinctive gown, or badge, in Court, distinguishing them from suitors and spectators, and making their calling a marked one, is another element, which tends to decrease the respect of the community, for the profession. In the administration of justice, the factitious influences are very great, in awakening and holding the respect of the community. The single judge sitting in his judicial robes creates a certain feeling of awe, and no matter how pusillanimous in figure or mind, he effectually controls the vast audience before him.

" So may the outward shows be least themselves
The world is yet deceived with ornament."

[1] Much has been written upon this subject, pro and con, in England, but I have felt it unnecessary to open it fully here. See ante, p. 81.

Here I shall end. I hope it is unnecessary to say that I love the profession, and have at heart the best interests of its members.

Apart from his individual employment, where his mind is naturally affected by the bias of an advocate, the lawyer is a character which the community should be interested in maintaining and not depreciating. His mind and training incline him to free and pure thought and independent judgment. That judgment is constantly called into exercise in every description of domestic and personal concern. Trained in the knowledge of human nature, when he enters the field of jurisprudence and politics, his acts and opinions should be of the greatest value to the people. I would build up a race of pure lawyers, as far removed from commercialism as possible. The country needs such a class more than ever. The distinction between a federation of States and a Nationality, it seems to me, is growing dim, and necessarily the people are less interested in public questions. The Bar, in its pristine vigor, is the saving ingredient in the composition of a democratic system of government, permeating and vitalizing all its branches, and securing liberty, while it sometimes restrains it, in the interest of social and political happiness.

The freedom of some of my remarks will doubtless create antagonism in some minds. It will

probably be the strongest where the lawyer himself is the purest, and has had the least opportunity of actual contact with certain kinds of
practice, on a large scale. He will think that he
advocates the interest of the profession by denying the existence of its evils. With such I have
an entire sympathy. Long and many-sided experience and observation, however, convince me
of the truth of what I have written. Otherwise
I should not have written. The welfare of our
noble calling, is as dear to me, as the life of which
it has formed so large a part. I can pity the
temptations with which it abounds even while
I urge its reform. That reform is needed, in all
those respects, and for all those great purposes,
to which I have called attention, I must freely
maintain, and in the venerable language familiar
to us all, "Of this I put myself upon the country."